Escaping Anxiety
Along the Road to Spiritual Joy

ALBERT E. HUGHES, Lt Colonel USAF, M.S., M.P.M,

Pastoral Minister and Spiritual Director

and

RONDA CHERVIN, Ph.D.

Professor of Philosophy and Spirituality

En Route Books and Media, LLC
5705 Rhodes Avenue
St. Louis, MO 63109

Cover Design by TJ Burdick

LCCN: 2018931088

ISBN-10: 0-9996670-8-4
ISBN-13: 978-0-9996670-8-8

DEDICATION

For Shannon, Katie, and Martha

CONTENTS

An Essential Introduction

Al Hughes

"The kingdom of God is not a matter of eating and drinking, but of Justice, peace and the joy that is given by the Holy Spirit. Whoever serves Christ in this way pleases God and wins the esteem of men."
(Romans: 14:17)

Given the choice, which do you prefer: a life of constant joy? Or a life plagued with frequent, even constant anxiety? The answer is obvious, but you may be thinking, "Constant joy just can't be had in this life. That's not a realistic choice!" But it is! There is a route, a road to constant joy. Burdened with anxiety, you yet may travel on.

Escaping Anxiety Along the Road to Spiritual Joy is a book that came out of my spiritual direction of an obsessively anxious directee. In successive chapters called sessions, we will show you how to escape from obsessive anxiety. We will walk you up the road to spiritual joy.

But we need to be specific. What do we mean by

joy? What do we mean by anxiety? By constant joy, we mean a state of peace and happiness, regardless of what else is going on in your life or around you, good or bad. Not giddiness, not elation, not alcohol or drug induced or even induced by happy news, but a constant state of peace, joy and happy acceptance regardless of circumstance.

By anxiety, we do not mean worry or concern in all its forms. Problems of life, daily problems, good news and bad news still will crop up demanding solutions. No, we mean that obsessive, nameless anxiety defined by Webster, thus:

> "...apprehensive uneasiness of mind often accompanied by physiological signs; doubt concerning the reality and nature of the threat, and by one's self doubt about one's capacity to cope with it."

Such anxieties crop up frequently, or even remain in an almost steady state, exhausting the emotions, draining away energy. Sound familiar? Among the clues which may suggest the presence of anxiety are –

1) constantly twirling a lock of hair,

2) wringing your hands or picking at your nails,

3) constantly pulling at one ear or the other,

4) absent mindedly rubbing your chin or face frequently;

5) or more radical and obvious or odd manner-

isms; little habits that make no sense.

Webster's "physiological signs."

The person afflicted with obsessive anxiety knows something is wrong but cannot express exactly what is wrong or its causes and knows not its cure; he or she cannot "name the beast" and accomplish a cure unaided. As you will see even from the first session, I will begin with a "fishing expedition," listening carefully and above all, watching non-verbal responses: listening for the ultimate cause of directee anxiety.

This book provides an almost unheard of opportunity to see the inner-workings of spiritual direction. Spiritual direction, otherwise, is conducted in strict confidence as the directee unburdens her secret inner life. We are not aware of any other such work, but this directee declares her life an open book for your benefit.

Each session begins with an explanation of purpose and/or method by me, Al Hughes, the Spiritual Director; followed by an accurate, reconstructed discourse with the directee, Ronda Chervin. Further on, our discussions may be replaced by alternating her journal entries with my responses or commentary. At the end of each session, you will find questions to help your understanding or spark your own group discussions.

The Art of Spiritual Direction

Spiritual direction is an art, not a science. In

general, science draws *inductive* inferences from multiple external measurements of similar objects which somehow can be "seen" and measured. The spiritual director is dealing in an *intuitive* way with an "object," which he cannot see or measure: the internal disposition of another person's soul. In some circumstances, he may employ published insights of psychology, but Christian spirituality pre-dates modern psychology by centuries – and calls upon the unseen God as referent example and power. The spiritual director operates routinely where few psychologists dare to go!

Further, while the artist paints an image on his own canvas which corresponds to his own mental image, the spiritual director tries to impress God's own image of *what ought be* in a manner which encourages another "artist" voluntarily to write a similar image on his own "canvas," his own soul: while erasing the deficient image already resident there. Now, let us, Spiritual Director and Directee, introduce ourselves in some detail. First of all, how does one, in this case did I, become a Spiritual Director? Then following, how did Ronda find me? And who is she?

Albert E. Hughes, M.S, M.P.M., Spiritual Director

I became a spiritual director by the most circuitous of routes: beginning with a baccalaureate in electrical engineering and an Air Force commission. I graduated with a Master of Science in Systems Management (with distinction) at the Air Force Institute of Technology in 1976. The following year I took command of Antigua Air Station, West Indies.

During the second year of my command, beginning in November, 1978, I had several mystical encounters with Christ, with an angel (just one) and with the Holy Spirit. I was propelled through mystical encounters from agnosticism to a baptized, Charismatic (Pentecostal) Catholic in eleven weeks! (My first book, *Paradise Commander,* has all the details.)

My wife, Jeannie, a lifelong Catholic, had a similar, earlier experience with the Holy Spirit. In unity after my encounter, we took vows of unconditional obedience to the will of God. (*Do not do that casually!* The Lord takes that vow very seriously! We later found religious history on the consequences of that vow.) God asked me to retire quite early from the Air Force (opposed to my own desires), then led me under obedience to a master of pastoral ministry (M.P.M,) and a 25-year practice as a Catholic catechist, retreat master and evangelist. The Holy Spirit knew me better than I knew myself!

In 1994, I graduated from the Spiritual Directors School at the Monastery of the Risen Christ in San Luis Obispo, California. Still later, after our third move under obedience to Corpus Christi, I was a Dean at Our Lady of Corpus Christi and published four books relating our encounters with the living God and

His gifts of insight. (Read my other books: *Paradise Commander; Saint Jeannie's Shiny Black Shoes; Buddy, Can You Spare a 'Digm?; Why I Am Still a Catholic* – all published by Goodbooks Media.)

In truly living according to my vow of unconditional obedience, I have been granted that grace of constant spiritual joy spoken of in Scripture; a joy based in consistent acceptance of things that cannot be changed, detachment from the temptations of Christ and from my own will in the normal course of events, and the development of a life of unconditional charity. All this will be defined and explained in due course.

You can't lead another where you have never been. I know the way to constant spiritual joy, so my mission as a Spiritual Director with regard to this book is to do what I can to help open you to a consistent level of grace-filled joy.

+

Now, as to Ronda. While I was a Dean at Our Lady of Corpus Christi, we taught down the hall from each other. It was in her writers group that I first began seriously to write. Recently, our friendship was re-energized when Ronda retired to Corpus Christi.

The Directee, Ronda Chervin, Ph.D.

Coming from a totally atheistic, Jewish background, I never thought there was such a thing as a human spirit, much less a Holy Spirit, until my 20th year. With the friendship of Catholics, studies and miracles, by the time I was 21, I certainly was on a spiritual journey.

A very general definition of spirituality is "the way to God." Since all my Catholic friends who followed the great philosopher and spiritual writer Dietrich Von Hildebrand were Benedictine Oblates (lay people linked with a Benedictine monastery), my first approach to spirituality was Benedictine. The center of my prayer life was daily Mass and the Liturgy of the Hours. My spiritual director was my godfather, Balduin Schwarz, a disciple of Von Hildebrand.

Later, a wife and mother of my small twin daughters, I happened to meet a woman at Church whose spirituality was Marian devotional. She introduced me to the rosary.

A huge expansion of my spiritual life came with the experience of the charismatic gifts of the Holy Spirit. As I used to put it before that, I tried to stand on tippy toes to reach up to the heavens. After those graces, I knew that Jesus was also inside my soul each moment, and I began to pray to him in a more heart to heart way. That is not to say that my previous mentors didn't also pray heart to heart to Jesus, but somehow, I didn't.

My spiritual director was a Jesuit priest at Loyola Marymount University where I was teaching philosophy. His emphasis was problem solving through discernment. This is because I have always been much stronger on insight into truth in itself than on seeing how God might be leading me in big and little decisions.

It was at this time that writing Catholic books and speaking at conferences, workshops and retreats became a part of my spiritual journey shared with students and general readers.

The next leap on my spiritual journey came about when I made a consecration to the Immaculate Heart of Mary. A replica of the statue of Our Lady of Fatima was brought to our home. When I prayed that her heart come into my heart, of a sudden I was ushered into contemplative prayer. This took the form of frequent interior (not audible) words in the heart, many poetic images and very occasional but powerful exterior visions. As well, I corresponded every day with a Jewish convert to the Catholic Faith, Charles Rich, a lay contemplative. (See my website at www.rondachervin.com – click on Friends of Charles Rich for more about this extraordinary mystic.)

Writing many books about the saints increased my deep desire to grow in holiness in spite of my very evident awful faults, especially explosive anger.

A quantum leap occurred when I became a widow more than 20 years ago. I tried many ways of life after that, but I finally settled on becoming a dedicated widow, i.e., a widow who makes a private promise not to remarry, but to live for Jesus and His Church.

With Jesus as a second bridegroom, I felt myself being led into a different mansion of the Church – where with an "undivided heart" I could commune with Jesus in a spousal union.

During all the decades of my life, I often benefitted from psychological counseling as well as spiritual direction. I am so, so grateful for all those mentors.

In my late 70's, I thought it would be smooth sailing ahead until the great moment when I would leave this earth and see Jesus face to face. But I suddenly found myself with a new obstacle to holiness: excessive anxiety.

God provided me just the spiritual director I needed to help me. Here is how that happened.

It was 2017. I just retired from full-time teaching as a philosophy professor. This watershed in my life came with a change of location from Cromwell, CT, to Corpus Christi, TX. "I need a new spiritual director here to help me get through the last decade(s) of my life!" I thought. Happily, one of my old friends in Corpus Christi is a lay spiritual director. On the way back from the airport, I asked Al Hughes to be my spiritual director. He laughed. (Probably knew what he was getting into.) Al tried to turn the tables on me, suggesting I should be directing him! Then he agreed.

How to Proceed?

We can suggest three classes of worry: worry about the inevitable, worry about what can be mitigated, and worry about that which is vague or unnamable.

Example of the inevitable: death, or imminent death of a dear one. The fact of death rightly approached should not be a subject of worry. Nothing can be done about death, itself. However, you likely will have sorrow, which lessens over time, and *concerns*: notifications, funeral arrangements, flowers, hospice, doctor or nurse issues or discussions, etc. It is right, normal and prudent to have such *concerns*.

Example of that which may be mitigated: damage from hurricanes. It is right and prudent here in Corpus Christi to be *concerned* at the approach of a hurricane in the western Gulf. Mitigations are called for. We board up, seal up, tie up, shut down and get out. Go to grandma's house in Kalamazoo! Not to worry! We have taken care of our *concerns* to the extent possible.

The point is, concerns regarding inevitable and mitigatable issues will pass; you have a responsibility to take action to the extent necessary and possible.

But unnamed anxieties persist; obsessive, vague, never passing. The person is unable to recognize the cause – name the beast, cannot respond; cannot resolve the issue without guidance. Concerns pass;

anxieties hang around. There are three ways to kill an anxiety; only one way to gain constant spiritual joy.

+

Step 1. There are three ways to kill anxiety: pills, psychology, or Papa. If you or others suspect a medical problem such as clinical depression, see your doctor. Prescribed pills can make the hit on such anxiety.

A good psychologist can prescribe for clinical depression as well and can diagnose particular anxieties due to behavioral problems; but only Papa will get you away from anxiety *permanently* and all the way to the grace of spiritual joy, *if you let Him!*

Step 2. This is where I, Al, started in my spiritual direction of Ronda: fishing for the bitter root judgment by way of conversation; piercing, sometimes painful questions, confrontation and careful observation. Fishing is a good analogy. Bitter roots are deep in the subconscious and need to be coaxed to the surface. The hooks of tough questioning can be painful.

Bitter root judgment: an unrecognized, subconscious, negative understanding of reality learned in childhood: will include self-blame, or negative self-judgment. It is a paradigm – an unrecognized pattern of thought, a hidden, false assumption about oneself. The cure?

Get help -> find it -> rebuke it -> challenge it ->

11

replace it with a positive opposite.

In Ronda's case, it took seven sessions to pull up that root.

Step 3. There is only one way to a lifetime cure and a move to constant spiritual joy; come to Papa! Abba! You are going to have to do things His way. Starting with detachment.

Detachment: an ascetic indifference to wealth, power and the easy life ("good fortune"). These three are Jesus' temptations in the desert. He rejected them; you must do the same. *Where your heart is, there will your treasure be.* Not absolute indifference, but enlightened and with a just sense of proportion; recognizing their difference in kind and their unimportance relative to that which determines the eternal destiny of the human being.

But what about detachment from your own will?

Detachment of will is the hardest, most necessary, and most meritorious – it is a control issue! Yours or His? The appropriately detached person leaves himself unreservedly in God's hands, "not as I will, but as thou wilt." (From *A Catholic Dictionary*, Donald Attwater, Gen. Ed.)

That's tough to consider, but consider this. If you are actually detached even from your own will, *there is nothing left to be anxious about!*

Step 4. With true detachment comes true **obedience**, two sides of the same coin. Recall that Jesus summarized the Old Testament commandments with a simple command, *Love God and your neighbor as yourself.* What exactly does it mean to love God whom we cannot see? Here is one of the most important and most overlooked passages in the New Testament. Jesus *defines* love of God!

> *They who have my commandments and keep them are those who love me; and those who love me will be loved by my Father, and I will love them and reveal myself to them.* (John 14:21)

Obedience to God *is* love of God. That simple. To obey well requires some level of detachment!

Step 5. Unconditional Charity: The last step before Spiritual Joy. Rid yourself of all prejudice, love all with prudence: affirm, build up, cast out all fear.

Step 6. Spiritual Joy: A graced state of constant peace and charity. Fruit of the Holy Spirit. *Not a virtue distinct from charity, but an act or effect of charity (Love).* St Thomas.

Step 7. En-joy. You have reached a level few reach. You have conquered yourself and given yourself as a gift to God. And oh, by the way. You have traveled the road not only to joy, but toward holiness.

+

As we begin, please join us in Ronda's prayer.

"Holy Spirit, only you know how many people in this world are riddled with obsessive anxiety, some even crippled by it. Yet, Jesus came to bring peace. You, Holy Spirit, inspired your servant, Al Hughes, to let you replace his anxieties with constant joy. By means of our writing may your peace and joy flow out into our hearts and into the hearts of all who read *Escaping Anxiety Along the Road to Spiritual Joy*."

"Faith makes nothing impossible; renders meaningless such words as anxiety, danger, and fear; the believer goes through life calmly and peacefully, with profound joy – like a child hand in hand with its mother."

- Venerable Charles de Foucauld

Session I

Anxiety: The Dismal Swamp

"For what I fear overtakes me,
and what I shrink from comes upon me,
I have no peace nor ease;
I have no rest, for trouble comes!"

Job 3:25

Stop! Did you read the introduction? It is vital you do so. All that follows is set up in the introduction. Without that opening introduction, little will be gained by proceeding. Read it!!! Then, please proceed.

<u>Spiritual Director's Introduction</u>: We begin by fishing for Ronda's alligators. By looking and listening and watching non-verbals, by listening to what is and is not said and by searching with carefully selected questions.

Please bear with me. Most of this fishing occurs in the first seven sessions. Our beginnings may seem disjointed at first reading but are essential to the process and leads to the catching of alligators – being root causes of Ronda's anger and obsessive anxiety. After we "catch" the alligators, we can move them out of the way – then we can lead Ronda along the road toward spiritual joy.

Indeed, out of my own south Louisiana background I used the image of fishing for alligators in our early discussions. As in fishing, we bait the hook and drop it in here, and there, and....

+

Over the table at the marina restaurant where we began meeting for spiritual direction, Ronda looked contrite. On a recent radio show she yelled at me! "I'm so sorry I yelled at you, Al; and right there in the middle of a panel discussion on the radio show, right there for all the panel and our audience to hear! I'm mortified. And now I'm worried you will reject me." Ronda was serious, fiddling with her fingernails, an almost constant habit.

She continued, "It wasn't wrong that I spoke the truth. As a long time philosophy professor, teaching the truth is what I do. I want to speak and teach the truth, and what you said, I just knew you were wrong. I had to say something! What's wrong was that I yelled at you!"

I, on the other hand, had not been upset. She likely was right, just loud! "Ronda, forget it. I have been yelled at by my father, by drill sergeants, by friends and opponents, even by my subordinates; by Colonels and Generals; even by Sir Wilfred, a British colonial Governor. People get excited! Emphatic! Didn't offend me a bit. How did you feel when you yelled at me?"

"I was just so angry, I .... Oh! I got it. You're trying to get me to focus not on the argument, but on the anger in my voice!"

"You did tell me the other day that you had your anger under control. What was that?" It was hard not to laugh.

Ronda deflected the question. "Well, not perfectly, but I used to have five fits a day before I got into Recovery International for anger, anxiety and depression. Remember, I used to lead one of those non-12-step groups when I was here in Corpus Christi years back; but on the radio show you were challenging something I knew for sure and you were wrong!" (Raising her voice, getting agitated.)

I had to keep things calm in the restaurant, so I admitted, "I've forgotten what I said that made you angry, but *you* are fiddling with your nails, again. Feeling a little anxious? Shall we talk about something else?"

Ronda finally smiled. "Don't try to patronize me. This is serious. I know your game. But the truth is important. That is what I am all about. It has to be right! Or...."

"That could be part of your problem," I interrupted.

"The truth?!"

"No, that that is what *you* are all about. I've been there, too. I reached a point where the Air Force was I; and I was the Air Force. Could hardly distinguish between the two, me and the Air Force. That came to a head when the Lord clearly asked me to retire early. That was anathema to me; though after a couple of months of evasion, I chose to honor my vow of obedience."

"So that's my problem? Too much at one with my work?"

There was my entre. I got prepared to fish in earnest. "That may be part of the problem or a symptom, but we are working on a puzzle, not a snapshot. You know life is complicated. We have only begun. So, while you are fiddling with your fingernails (again), here is a question for you to really worry. So, you were angry and yelled at me. And we have a reason that may or may not get to the bottom of your anger. The truth is important to you, so you spoke out forcefully. Why such vigor?"

Ronda was stopped cold. She really had to think about that, to dig deeper, one level further down. Her desire for truth could really help, now. She began, "I guess you were assaulting the truth, somehow? Truth is important, especially nowadays when there are a lot of people who seem to think that truth is whatever they want it to be."

"I was assaulting an abstract concept? Interesting. Didn't know I had that in me. Really? Do you think the concept felt any pain?"

"You're trying to be funny," Ronda laughed. "I got the point. It seemed like you were assaulting me. I had to defend myself."

"So you are the truth and the truth is you?"

"Maybe just like you and the Air Force. Things get all mixed up when you devote your life to something."

I threw in a little consolation, but really was fishing. "It's hard to remember you came to drain the swamp when you're up to your ass in alligators! Care to go a little deeper? (Pause) Let's see. So somehow by countering what you thought of was truth...did that seem like maybe relativism to you? Or that I was actually countering you? How did you feel?"

Ronda retorted, "I told you before that you are sardonic, but you are pushing on the door of sarcasm. I felt like I feel now, a little pained by your pressure."

"Caused by?" It was no time to be put off by her resistance. We were starting to get somewhere.

"Alright, you got me. It felt like you were rejecting the truth. Yes, and I could not separate rejection of the truth from rejection of me. Is that the point? Is that the root of my anger?"

"Don't know, we are just fishing now, fishing for alligators."

Ronda grinned. "Sooner or later you Louisiana boys get back to your roots, don't you?"

For a moment, I had a flashback to college days. "I did do a little alligator headlighting in the swamps east of Breaux Bridge with a classmate. One night around 2:00 am, we stocked the Student Union pond with a lively young two-foot alligator. That was a long time ago. Now, we are hunting a picture of an alligator on a puzzle; your alligator. We may have a few pieces of the puzzle. That's all."

I continued. "So, what we have now is a short stack of puzzle pieces, anger hiding anxiety hiding pain of real or anticipated rejection; and it is no wonder. I finished reading your autobiography *En Route to Eternity*.

"In summary, you and your twin were saturated in novels and in a family environment of seemingly *conditional* love, with competing and shifting alliances. Soaked in real and fictional drama. You even call yourself a drama queen. You had plenty of opportunities to experience real and imaginary rejections."

Ronda got defensive. "Yes, but it wasn't all rejection. My mother adored me. Even though, since she was an editor by trade, she critiqued everything I said incorrectly; she also beamed with pleasure every time I said anything smart or witty."

I had Ronda's autobiography with me, with post-its sticking out on some of the pages, ready for her mild protest. "In your book, it seems you lived in a steady state condition of repeated rejection by someone at all times. As you wrote on page 18, 'You could never know when angry rejection would replace loving delight.' And on the next page, '...atmosphere of deceit.' And again on page 25, 'I am very dependent.' On page 31, I found 'I believed that I was an evil person whom everyone would despise.' On the same page again, 'I had feelings of not fitting in.' Finally, on page 43, 'I developed a certain hardness.'

"Is that what you remember, now?"

Sadly, "Yeah, I wrote that."

It was time to share a real example of a woman I had helped years back in California. "Let me tell you about a woman who expected rejection because of one incident. She was four years old and deeply loved her dad, as he loved her. He went on a business trip. On the morning of his return he called. His wife put their four-year-old on the phone. Daddy said he loved her and was coming home that evening. He died in a plane crash that day. Daddy never came home.

"When I spoke at length with that little girl, then around age 42, she was on the verge of losing her third marriage. After several sessions, it turned out she pushed all men away, in fear of being rejected; based on that incident! As she said to me, remembering the perspective of a four-year-old, 'Daddy didn't really love me. No man could love me.' She had rejected three husbands in anticipation that, sooner or later, they would reject her! One rejection can be enough to cause continuing anxiety. What else might we find?

We ended the session on that note.

Here is how I, as Ronda's spiritual director summarize my insights during this session. At an intellecttual level, Ronda understands some of the elements of her problem. But it is one thing to know and very much another willingly and effectively to set aside lifetime attitudes and habits. She understands much and lightly characterizes herself accordingly, but "in the trenches" of day-to-day relations with others, even in the use of inanimate objects: examples – her computer, door locks, thermostats, etc. – the slightest difficulty or disagreement mushrooms into anxiety in expectation of disaster, often to the point of utter frustration and sudden anger. After nearly 80 years, she is well-accustomed to sniff out any opportunity to imagine personal rejection or presume any obstacle to be overwhelming.

For Personal Reflection and Group Sharing:

- What insights and experiences do you relate to in this first session?

Session II

Entering the Swamp

"Threaten the wild beast that dwells in the reeds."

Psalm 68: 30

Spiritual Director's Introduction: At the end of the first session I asked Ronda, as homework, to summarize feelings and insights she had coming out of our conversations. It would be of no use to proceed past her current understanding without clarifying as needed.

This session was more or less free form, allowing Ronda to explore and relate her own memories and suspicions with only occasional comment from me. As do most fishermen, I was fishing for clues more or less in silence. Watching the rippling "waters" of her unfolding emotions, revealing more in her face even than in her words.

+

25

"First of all," Ronda offered, "since most of my rejections came from men, I want to thank you for being a healing man, a spiritual director and friend for me at this time of my life. I am in awe that you would take so much time to try to help me."

Ronda began by questioning the difference between concerns and anxieties. "Probably because I am a philosopher, I need to begin by sorting out types of anxiety. You briefly mentioned when we started that you do not mean by anxiety what you would call concerns, as in concerns about dangers that we can do something to avoid. For instance, if a hurricane is coming we board up the house.

"So then, here is my question. Does that mean that anxiety about a possibly catastrophic illness of my adult daughter is excessive just because I can't do anything for her; only pray for her? It sounds as if you are blaming me for absolutely natural human anxieties that no one can avoid!"

"I also said 'inevitable,'" I responded to Ronda. "And the doctors *are* doing something to mitigate her cancer. Chemo or radiation or whatever.

"I chose to invoke the term 'concern' to distinguish between legitimate concerns over actual passing issues that can be mitigated or are inevitable and your seemingly unending state of unsubstantiated anxiety in expectation that you will be rejected again.

"Your own autobiography is a record of perceived rejections, but there is no evidence that you will be rejected by anyone again. Unless, as you wrote of your childhood, you really believe, despite your incredible professional record and horde of admirers, you still are an 'evil person whom everyone will despise.'"

Ronda became a bit evasive; she was picking at her fingernails again. "No, definitely not! (Pause) Well, maybe just a little?" Quickly, she moved on.

"Oh, here's another one. Suppose underlying the anxiety about this daughter's illness is the fear that if she dies of it, even though her sister might take care of me, it is still one daughter who couldn't. I may not find someone to take care of me in my old age. Others, not biologically related to me, could more likely reject me and I would have a horrible last few years – pain, neglect, and loneliness. Maybe even go out of my mind!"

"Exactly! Yes! But is that real? Actual? Pre-ordained?

Ronda suggested, "I think it would be good to have a rundown of some of the rejections of childhood and adulthood that I can remember. The rejection that I clearly remembered at different times when I was in psychotherapy was this. When my father left our little family of four, my twin sister and I were eight years old. He contributed some money for a while. My mother had been a career woman before staying home to take care of us twins, but she clearly needed to find a job soon."

"Did she talk about fear of poverty?" I interrupted.

"Never!" Ronda exclaimed. I just surmised later, trying to analyze my own insecurity; she must have felt anxious and that maybe I picked up on this."

Testing, I threw this in. "Psychologists say that the kids of divorced parents blame themselves and feel rejected."

"I certainly didn't consciously feel this, but I do remember feeling jealous of my father's new wife and her teen-age daughter. That might be caused by a sense of rejection, wouldn't it?"

"Yes."

Ronda wanted to continue from her written list of rejections. "The first few weeks of public school in New York City, my twin-sister Carla and I looked different than other students because we were brought up wearing overalls, and the other girls in the class wore pretty dresses. The school administrators insisted our mother buy us skirts and blouses, but I think we felt immediately that we didn't fit in."

"Did you feel rejected as children at that school?" Al asked.

"Generally, I would say we were some place in the

middle – never in the popular clique but never ostracized either." Ronda swiftly described some other rejections. "Boyfriends! My first one went to a college out of town while I was still in High School. After a half-year away, he stopped writing letters every day and hooked up with another girlfriend whom he eventually married."

"The second boyfriend I had a love affair with in college. We both certainly were in love, but he was looking to marry a woman in his field of study whose father was a big-shot in the medical profession. A good job for him would be waiting if he married her, instead of me. So, after a year of our torrid romance he broke it off."

Looking sympathetic, Al asked: "What did you feel when he did that?"

"I was devastated. With my atheistic bohemian family background, I didn't actually believe in marriage. So, I just assumed that if a man and woman loved each other very much they would stick together."

"But you did get married when you became a Catholic."

"As you have read in my autobiography. As a Catholic, I did find a man who wanted to marry."

Ronda looked back down at her list of rejections

and read this to Al: "To make a long story short, early in our marriage my husband did something I thought constituted a big rejection for me, was a betrayal of our love. I intuited that this happened. It seemed to me that everything was finished. But since I was a Catholic who didn't believe in divorce and we already had two children, I forgave him in my mind, but still felt totally rejected. Years later, I realized that in turn I rejected him for decades.

"It took a healing service of unconditional forgiveness for married couples, for me to really forgive him from the heart. Many decades later someone told me that when she asked my husband, Martin, whether she should make a certain choice, he replied, 'Don't do it. You could hurt the person you love the most in a way that you can never make up.'

"And just now, it is clear to me that he was not rejecting me at all in that sin. He was just tempted. How different our marriage would have been had we gone to a marriage counselor right away. I think I wanted, instead, to punish him by rejecting him in my heart.

"Now, Al, having written about these rejections, and seeing also that all my life I anxiously feared rejection, mostly from men, I am wondering what you really are trying to teach me. You say that one need have no excessive anxiety at all, in spite of past rejections. What do you really mean?"

"If I may be brusque, it is like you have spent your whole life to now, surrounded by real and imagined alligators and you are spending the rest of your life anxiously imagining that you might be eaten.

"The answer may be, confront the alligator: as my wife once did to conquer her fear of Florida palmetto bugs (thumb size large roaches). She caught one in a jar, put a lid on it and put the jar on the window sill over her kitchen sink. She had to watch that bug every day. She actually got to liking the thing and let it go outside! Don't think she named it, though.

"I am convinced there are more puzzle pieces we haven't found yet. Not one alligator in our picture puzzle, but several. For now, let's confront the alligator we have found with a little experiment.

"As homework mark three full columns on an empty page. If you have to, tape another page to the bottom. In the left column list every living person you know personally who you think loves you. In the middle column list all your good personal attributes, degrees, professional accomplishments, current works and hopes for the rest of your life. In the right column, list all whom you think you have rejected. That's all. Bring it to the next session."

"But why...?" Ronda asked.

"Just do it. We will figure out the next step next week. But be thorough in your lists."

For Personal Reflection and Group Sharing:

- Do you have a fear of rejection? If so, can you describe your experiences of rejection?

Session III

The Swamp at Dusk:
Troubled Waters

"If you find yourself in an argument, stop! Define your terms. Most arguments are over word definitions, not the facts of the matter."

Anon

Spiritual Director's Introduction: I, Al, knew that! I learned that in freshman engineering orientation – the first day of class, early September 1958! Our instructor told us that. And carefully at the beginning of spiritual direction, I defined terms with Ronda.

But I did not repeat that concerns are legitimate, based in a reality which eventually passes. Whereas, "anxiety," as we will deal with it, is that form of worry that hangs around indefinitely, mostly unnamed and with cause vague or unknown.

Nor did I recognize the full extent of Ronda's focus

33

on "concern" for her seriously ill daughter in another State. Wrought with worry, she did not distinguish between terms. Hardly! At my introductory comment, this session blew up in my face. It took much of the session to calm Ronda down and re-introduce the distinction I had made between "concern" and "anxiety."

But Ronda's anger was information, too; and I had only begun to fish for the root cause of her anxiety. Clearly, while she had not incorporated into her habitual thinking the distinction between concern and anxiety, which I had crafted so carefully, my intent remained to continue our conversations in more or less free form until I was assured I was hearing the root of her anxiety and explosive anger.

+

We were just at the beginning of our Sunday-after-Mass session at a back table in the Citrus Bistro restaurant. Casually, I was talking about how when one gets healed of excessive anxiety the pains of life become little.

Ronda, getting louder and louder, boomed out for much of the restaurant to hear, "That's crazy. Right now, my daughter is in the hospital in great pain. In empathy with her, how could my pain become 'LITTLE'?!"

At my calm down gesture, she said in a broadcast

voice, "I'm not YELLING!" *Then* she quieted just a bit, but her face was transmitting anger. She was *blowing her stack*. If you are not familiar with that phrase, it comes from steam railroad days. At the start of a long uphill climb, the engineer would blast steam up the smoke stack. That would increase the air velocity through the firebox, generate steam faster, and provide power to get over the peak of the hill. Ronda was steamed!

"You think my worry about my daughter, who's desperately sick in the hospital, in constant pain, is a LITTLE matter!?"

Quickly I tried to change the subject: "We'll get to 'little' a little later. For now, let's talk about the homework assignment." Still agitated, Ronda whipped out her page of notes, with three columns marked on a sheet of paper. The left column listed all her living friends and relatives; she had listed 50 in all. The middle column listed all her good attributes, degrees and accomplishments, which were many. The right column was a much shorter list of those friends and associates whom she remembered having rejected.

Intentionally, she had not been told the reason for the exercise. We read off the center column: friendliness, responsibility...and much more; her collegiate degrees and accomplishments, which were many. After a short review, I handed her a red pen. "Here; now circle one of the names in the left column to signify that this person has rejected you."

Bad timing. Ronda, already having spent weeks in "concern" about her daughter, went right to the first name on the list; her very sick daughter. Oblivious to what was coming next, I continued, "Now look at the middle list. Your good attributes, degrees and accomplishments. Which of your good attributes, degrees and accomplishments have you lost because of that rejection?"

Flustered and upset, Ronda replied: "What do you mean? If my daughter rejected me totally, I would lose something HUGE!" She thought I was be-"little"-ing her whole relationship with her daughter!

She continued. "I am sure, Al, that you are familiar with the Jewish philosopher Martin Buber and his book *I and Thou,* so popular in the second half of the 20th century."

"Yes."

Ronda continued in her lecture style: "The point I want to focus on is Buber's moving away from our individualistic way of thinking of the human person in terms of accomplishments, talent, etc., to see that part of the "I" is the person who emerges in relationship. These he calls I-Thou relationships in contrast to I-it relationships such as the "I" that uses a can opener (an "it.")

"So, when I am rejected by someone who is a

"thou" for me, the "I" that emerged in that relation-ship is deeply hurt, sometimes permanently. As in, if my daughter rejected me, the part of me that is motherly to her is no longer able to operate."

Raising her voice again, Ronda ended her lecture: "That is not LITTLE, Al!"

I thought, but dared not say at that point, "That's what I deserve for going up against a philosophy professor. I read Buber, too. But that was maybe 30 years ago. Didn't see that one coming. But the real problem is that we are talking past each other. I started this session in the context of her irrational *anxiety*, but she is fixed on her rational *concern* for her daughter." Buber was not addressing anxiety.

Eventually Ronda half-conceded the point. "All right, I got it. I don't lose my whole selfhood with my talents and virtues, even if my daughter rejects me. Probably, certainly, really, just for a small period of time."

"Ronda, it is not about your concern regarding immediate problems, but about the inner, seemingly constant feelings of anxiety that have been with you since childhood. You have admitted that yourself. That alligator may be bigger than I thought. Anxiety, or your underlying pain resulting from fear of rejection may be addictive. You carry the constant assumption that something is about to go wrong, though you know not what. That is what we are trying to heal."

I lightly mentioned the third column of her homework; that she also was guilty of rejecting others, and then transitioned with a sip of tepid coffee.

Ronda tried to move with the moment. "But isn't there always pain? Isn't that part of life? There always is pain!"

"Often, Ronda, often. But no, not always. Your constant pain is self-generated. You have feared rejection constantly for so long that that fear has become pain, itself. If your pain is constant, you have created that anxiety, yourself. That is the alligator I am fishing for.

"Hmmmmm!" Ronda picked at the skin around her nails more forcefully. "I don't agree that most pain has to be self-induced. I actually think that those who don't experience pain of some sort or another are either indifferent, callous, or so numbed out by pain they have to be in denial. I mean..." I motioned for Ronda to lower her voice. She continued, "Heck, we should be in pain just because of all the sin and suffering in the world; not that we can't have joy and pain simultaneously; as in joy because of God and the Faith, but pain because of the way life is on earth."

"You're getting defensive, Ronda. We will talk about all that another time. There is a joyful, pain relieving answer, but right now I want to stick with your self-inflicted pain.

I continued, "How 'bout a personal example. Because my father was physically present, but generally ignored me in my childhood, I spent many years in a subconscious search for my father. It affected my adult life negatively in that, unaware, I was trying to attach fatherhood first to professors, then to senior USAF officers. Those men neither recognized my search for what it was, nor were they prepared to be surrogate fathers for me. From their perspective, they were not rejecting me, had no idea what was going on in my mind, subconsciously; but from repeated experiences I expected to be rejected, therefore concluded time and again that I was rejected.

"I was a Major, for goodness sakes, before I read about that effect of a psychologically absent father and realized what I was doing. I was able fully to correct that tendency only when my actual father died. Even then only because I read about that psychological problem. Still, I would never have associated that tendency with anxiety or pain. Nor was it constant, but only periodic. Once fully understood and mitigated, my self-reliance strengthened. I still think about it occasionally, but only in the context of renewing my understanding of the matter.

"Are you searching for someone, Ronda?"

+

A day or two later, I asked that question again in an e-mail. Ronda responded immediately. "Of course! My father left us when my twin and I were only eight years old!"

I then assigned homework for later discussion.

For Personal Reflection and Group Sharing:

- What leaped out at you from reading Session 3?

- Do you ever get defensive when anyone calls you on being excessively anxious?

Session IV
Turmoil on False Bayou

Martha was distracted by her many tasks.... But the Lord answered her, "Martha, Martha, you are anxious and distracted by many things; there is need of only one thing needed."

Luke 10:40

<u>Spiritual Director's Introduction</u>: The day after the last session, by e-mail I assigned homework for discussion during this session. Periodically during the week Ronda was to read a treatise "On Spiritual Perfection" by Diadophis of Photice, bishop. Diadochus was dealing with the anxiety and excess busyness of his audience, so long ago. His comments would hit Ronda head on, revealing the folly of her anxiety.

But first, I had to take care of some old business, head on. Seated at the usual table in the Bistro, I wanted to hold off the session until after brunch. Ronda agreed, but her face suggested impatience. She

41

was anxious to bring up her own leftover issue from before. Late in the meal she finally said, "Shall we?"

Nodding assent, I moved my plate to an unoccupied space on a far corner of the table, and said, "First thing, today, we need to close the book on our conflict that erupted last week. We both were emphatic in our discussion, but we were talking past each other on separate subjects.

"Early on, we distinguished between irrational, obsessive *anxiety* as a habitual anticipation and fear of future, often unnamed problems that likely never would happen, and *concern* over real problems that are inevitable or can be mitigated. I was talking about irrational, obsessive anxiety and you were fixed on real concern for your seriously ill daughter."

"I know, Al, and besides, she is much better, now. But you also said that if my pain of anxiety is constant, it's because I keep feeding it. You said I created that pain, myself!" Ronda's voice was starting to rise, irritated at remembering my accusation. She stopped just short of her lecture style.

"I think, Al, I am still bogged down on the issue of types of pain. There can be underlying pain because of all the sufferings in the world including that of our loved ones and our own sufferings. Think of John-Paul II. From videos of him on TV and in other photos and from reading long, long biographies of him, I would say that he had constant pain from all the evils in the world.

"Of course, he had lots of joy, simultaneously, which came out especially in videos when he was greeting people. Sure, he could be joyful, but he almost always looked like he was in pain. You could see it in his face. His pain was constant! Those who say they aren't in constant pain along with some joy are either indifferent, callous, or so numbed out by pain that they are in denial!"

I was careful not to say, "Even a full professor can throw a red herring into the net," though it would have been factual! What I did say was...

"Whatever is true about JPII, there is no evidence that he had constant, obsessive anxiety about un-named or vague and unlikely happenstances, Ronda. He had a lot of responsibility. Maybe he was just con-centrating on the reality of the present moment – which is exactly the approach of a truly holy man. He is a canonized saint, isn't he?"

Ronda looked thoughtful, but did not respond. We transitioned to the intended topic of the day, "On Spiritual Perfection" by Diadochus of Photice, bishop. (I have a lecture style, too, don't you know?)

"First point: Diadochus wrote in part, *The light of true knowledge makes it possible to discern without error the difference between good and evil. (It follows that) ...therefore, we must maintain great*

stillness of mind, even in the midst of our struggles.
Then by analogy, he extends the thought. *A tranquil
sea allows the fisherman to gaze right to its depths.
No fish can hide there and escape his sight. The
stormy sea, however, becomes murky when it is
agitated by the winds. The very depths...the sea now
hides."*

I got emphatic, accusatory! "Ronda, your sea, your
mind, is constantly being agitated, made murky by
obsessive anxiety. You are constantly worried and
scheming about some vague, unknown future rejection by somebody; anybody! You are constantly, anxiously plotting and scheming to outflank unknown,
unlikely future rejections."

"I know, Al, but I am so worried that I might be
incapacitated, or even lose my mind, and there will be
no one to take care of me. I've reached 80, for
goodness sakes. Most of my friends are as old as I am,
and my close relatives who might care for me are
scattered all over the Nation, from coast to coast. And
they need help, too!"

"Of course. And that is why, among other schemes,
you plot and dream of a religious lay community that
will take care of you 'till the end. I've know you for
years, Ronda. That scheme is old news and you are
still at it! You have mentioned it several times since
returning to Corpus Christi. It ain't gonna happen!
You need to let go of that scheme and trust God!"

Continuing, "<u>Second point</u>: again according to Diadochus, *Only the Holy Spirit can purify the mind...so by every means, but especially by peace of soul, we must try to provide the Holy Spirit with a resting place. Then we shall have the light of knowledge shining within us at all times, and it will show up for what they are all the dark and hateful temptations that come from demons,...exposure to this holy and glorious light will also greatly diminish their power. This is why the Apostle says: Do not stifle the Spirit.*

Then picking up the thread of the Apostle and Diadocus' thought, "Ronda, you've known Jesus for near sixty years; you've <u>know</u> the Holy Spirit as a charismatic Catholic for many of those years; and you have been working in the vineyard for a long time. But in this matter of self-inflicted anxiety, you have asked the Holy Spirit to sit in the back while you drive through endless mental mazes, scheming your way toward the back gate of the vineyard."

"I know, Al, but my future is a real problem! I could lose my mind and wind up wandering in the street somewhere! Who will protect me?"

"It's one thing, Ronda, to <u>know</u> we should and say we do trust God, another to actually incorporate total trust and let go of useless anxieties. It is a simple and most difficult matter to actually trust. The difficulty is to give up on one's control (which ultimately is an illusion, anyway) and trust God with hope for future outcomes."

"Diadochus' third point: ...*so when our mind is strong and free from all anxiety, it is able to taste the riches of divine consolation...as Saint Paul says: My prayer is that your love may increase more and more in knowledge and insight, and so enable you to choose what is best.*

Initially, I did not want, directly, to bring up the subject of spiritual detachment; it was too early to deal with head on. But Ronda already knew of detachment in an intellectual way. And since detachment was the underlying subject evoked by Diadochus, I mentioned it in passing, as a move toward ending the session.

"Ronda, you know about the virtue of detachment. The fully detached person leaves himself unreservedly in God's hands, 'not as I will but as thou wilt'; he asks for nothing and refuses nothing. (As defined in *A Catholic Dictionary*, Donald Attwater, Gen Ed.) You trust God in many ways, but you are anxiously, obsessively trying to manage your own end game. That is a control issue, not surprisingly. You have perceived a need to manage and control your own life for many years.

"The other issue is that eight-year old in you, still calling out to your father as he abandoned your family, 'Look at me! I am real! Love me! Protect me!'

So, your many anxieties are focused on obsessive need to control and on panic avoidance of further rejection.

"A friend of mine says about anxiety, 'Anxiety is interest paid on a loan not received.'"

"Yes," Ronda said, "I've heard you say that before."

"OK, then here is your simple homework. STOP SCHEMING!

+

A day or two after this session, Ronda realized that we still may be talking past each other on the topic of pain. Her use of the word includes both physical and psychological or spiritual pain, i.e., sorrow. Sure enough, I use the word "pain" only in the physical context. Ronda suggested she would try to say sorrow when she meant sorrow.

Can Ronda resist scheming about her future? We shall see.

For Personal Reflection and Group Sharing:

- Do you make a distinction between underlying sorrow in your heart about the sins and sufferings in the world and self-induced pain from anxiety?

- Can you try to still your mind from excessively anxious thoughts so that you can better understand what God is trying to tell you?

- What is the biggest reason in your life right now that you think you have to be anxious about? How could greater trust in God help?

Session V

Running Amuck in the Muck

For what profit comes to a man from all the toil and anxiety of heart with which he has labored under the sun.

Ecclesiastes 1:3-4

<u>As no darkness can be seen by anyone surrounded by light, so no trivialities can capture the attention of</u> anyone who has his eyes on Christ. 'What can separate us from the love of Christ, which is in Jesus? Can affliction or distress?'

From a homily on Ecclesiastes by Saint Gregory of Nyssa

<u>Spiritual Director's Introduction</u>: First, a reminder, going forward. Neither these sessions with Ronda, nor the process of spiritual direction necessarily progress in lockstep with a hard outline of step by step pre-ordained directee improvements. This is not surgery, but an artistic endeavor trying one approach or another as the "light" changes in the directee's per-

ceptions: light to dark and back to light on an unpredictable schedule. Any artist in paint will tell you that things can get messy. As discussed in the intro:

While the artist with a pallet paints an image on his own canvas which corresponds to his own mental image, the spiritual director tries to express God's image of *what ought be*, in a manner which encourages another "artist," the directee, voluntarily to write a similar image on his own "canvas," his own soul: while erasing the deficient image already resident there. Like the painted picture on a canvas, the directee's "light" does not necessarily respond as the spiritual director desires, but sometimes flares ahead, then dims in a backslide. The process can get messy!

There were two clues occurring during and immediately after the same daily Mass. Ronda, our friend Jim, and I often attend daily Mass together, sitting up front on the right in the first pew. This time, Jim came up the side aisle after Mass had started; he sat five rows back.

After Mass, Jim and Ronda stopped behind my car in conversation. I got in, started the engine and flipped on the radio. Jim soon opened the other door opposite; Ronda opened the back door, opposite. Immediately, in a harsh tone she said, "You turned that radio on so you would not have to listen to me!" Jim and I laughed, thinking she was joking, until I turned and looked at her. She was dead serious, and accusatory.

In the ensuing conversation, it turned out that she seriously felt rejected by both of us. Me for the radio being on, Jim because he did not sit next to her during Mass! She confessed that her first thought was, "He must hate to sit next to me."

Jim quickly explained that he felt uneasy walking all the way down front after Mass had started; he was a little late sitting down and didn't want to be noticed walking up to the front pew.

And I explained that the radio was turned on when no one else was in the car, just to hear what program was on; I had no way of knowing how long they would talk, standing behind the car! Still, it took a few minutes for her to calm down.

+

When we met as usual Sunday, we reviewed Ronda's homework from the last session; to try to stop scheming about imaginary, unrealistic futures. But when we met for this session, Ronda expressed a need to review, to summarize what she understood from our previous work together. We still were dealing with her obsessive scheming and resultant anxiety; a long way from entering the road to spiritual joy.

"Al, even though often I thought you were exaggerating during these last few weeks, I find that your themes keep coming up over and over again, so that I cannot deny the truth you are trying to get across to me."

"Examples?" I responded, needing to know exactly where she actually was, not where I thought she might be. By the way, this is a general problem for thinkers and public speakers, especially professors, that they imagine that insight equals real change of heart in themselves, when it often doesn't.

Ronda went on, "First of all, I am trying to modify my language. So instead of automatically saying, 'I am worrying about this or that,' or 'I am anxious about this or that', I look first to see if the worry is a realistic concern. If it is, I say 'concern.' Concern is less inflammatory, less like a drama queen?"

"For sure," I encouraged her. "Tell me about a typical instance or two of this, as in?"

"As in, I had a terrible time replacing my lap top with a desk top computer since I don't understand tech well and readily get angry when a person helping me seems to just assume I will get his instructions easily. This time around I kept noticing that some of my fears were understandable 'concerns.' Other conclusions, such as thinking the new computer will never work, and I have to stop all my activities that depend on the computer and just sleep and eat and go to Mass and pray the rosary and never communicate with anyone again online; really did manifest excessive anxiety!"

I exclaimed, *"First name the beast!* Just like going to confession. In this case, recognize the alligator. Confirming her discovery, "I did say that having concerns is perfectly legitimate, but you easily move from concern to excessive anxiety about imaginary, unlikely outcomes. Your discovery is the first step to change, to freeing yourself from obsessive anxiety!"

Ronda gave herself a congratulatory smile and continued, "Now, on the rejection thing, Al, I am beginning to see how obsessive this really is! It is constant! You know I wrote a book titled *Healing of Rejection: A Survivor's Guide,* and you even got a lot out of reading that book. But that was about blatant rejections such as when a parent outright rejects his own son or a boss rejects his employee friends, examples I used in my book. It also has examples of romantic rejections.

"Now I see it! That I think I am being rejected because of trivialities, ludicrous things; even with friends like you who have shown me so much care in my troubles."

I had to laugh. Saint Gregory used the same word in this session's starting quotation, "trivialities!" "You got it! That sure was a triviality when you thought my car radio was on so that I did not have to listen to you. Noticing excessive anxiety is necessary as a good move toward opening yourself to trust and God's grace; not to mention it makes common sense."

Before closing I asked her about her homework from session four – to stop scheming about unlikely future outcomes. That has to stop if she ever wants to attain peace of mind. She can't let those fantasies roll along unchecked.

"Yeah, okay," she began, "So I saw that it is not excessive to plan for my daughter's visit next month, but to scheme how a fan I just met on a radio interview might take care of me in my old age is absurd!"

"Right," I confirmed. "The more outlandish the scheme, the more it will make you obsessively anxious, because the outcome certainly is uncertain and you can't possibly know if you will even like this woman, much less plan to move in with her and have her take care of you! You wind up obsessing on unfeasible schemes to make impossible dreams possible."

I dropped Ronda off at her apartment, without assigning any home work. As I drove away, the light came on.

SHE THINKS THAT EVERYTHING SHE SEES OR HEARS IS ABOUT HER! SELF CONSCIOUSNESS RUN AMUCK! THAT'S WHAT MAKES THE EARLY TEEN YEARS SO DIFFICULT. SHE IS STUCK IN THAT REPEATING ANXIETY NORMATIVE TO THE

EARLY TEEN YEARS!

For Personal Reflection and Group Sharing:

- As you read this session, what examples of excessive anxiety or scheming about the future that Ronda gave remind you of any forms of outward or inward behavior you tend toward?

- What observations of Al about Ronda's syndromes could be helpful to you?

Session VI

Roots in the Shallows

*Could anything remain hidden in me? I would only
be hiding you from myself. I am displeased with
myself. I have renounced myself and chosen you,
recognizing that I can please neither you nor myself
unless you enable me to do so.*

From the Confessions of Saint Augustine

Spiritual Director's Introduction: Children are
great observers and poor interpreters: interesting, obvious, true. The child sees and hears an event clearly,
but what is remembered is the interpretation of the
event *as it applies to the life of the knowledge-hungry
child.* If the event is interpreted as a negative experience by a child – and if it is repeated in thought or
in actuality sufficiently – the interpretation becomes
an established subconscious understanding of reality.
As often happens, the interpretation may include self-
blame and a negative self-judgment: the child may
grow up acting out of an unrecognized self-accusing

bitter root judgment.

Example: this spiritual director grew up in a standard middle class American family. My father was a good, honorable husband; but emotionally distant, seemingly disinterested in his son. Quality time with my father just didn't exist. Bitter root judgement? He did not love me and no one else could love me or even like me because I was physically ugly –the conclusion of a child. My high school pictures prove otherwise, but I remained in that belief, painfully shy and reclusive until I was 26, an Air Force Captain!

On hearing me give this example, Ronda responded with a look of compassion: "So sad. Well, now, Al, even at age seventy-six you look much more handsome than most men of your age! Let me describe you to our readers. Al is a 5' 8" man, trim, with white hair and short whiskers. He has blue eyes, often twinkling with amusement, but he thinks they are hazel. His typical expression is a kind of benign reflectiveness as he looks around himself in the Church or in the bistro where we take our lunches. He sees and evaluates everything. But when he zeros in on me in the spiritual direction session, his eyes are penetratingly incisive, especially when making a point he thinks I might reject. However, when he notices a stricken look of anxiety in my face, then comes an expression of compassionate love."

After two months, I had enough information to dig

for Ronda's bitter root judgment. Given her occasional bouts of explosive anger, I was able to use an image titled "Ronda's Childhood Volcano." Take a look at my diagram reading from the bottom up in sequence, then consider.

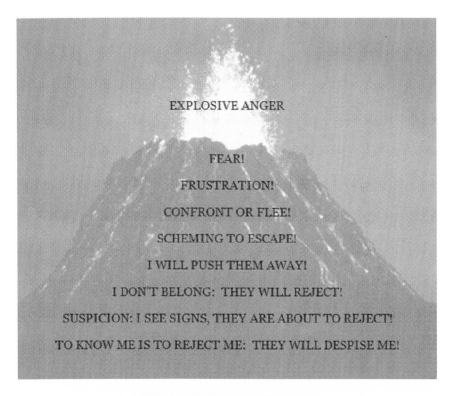

EXPLOSIVE ANGER

FEAR!

FRUSTRATION!

CONFRONT OR FLEE!

SCHEMING TO ESCAPE!

I WILL PUSH THEM AWAY!

I DON'T BELONG: THEY WILL REJECT!

SUSPICION: I SEE SIGNS, THEY ARE ABOUT TO REJECT!

TO KNOW ME IS TO REJECT ME: THEY WILL DESPISE ME!

RONDA'S CHILDHOOD VOLCANO

After the usual brunch, I showed her a very pleasant picture of herself from her autobiography: a lovely middle-aged lady with long, well combed hair, wearing a modest, yet attractive dress and a crucifix. She is smiling. "Tell me, what is wrong with this picture?"

She examined the picture closely, and then,

slightly peeved, said, "There is nothing wrong with that picture!"

"Right," I agreed. "Just a picture of a lovely woman who seems happy."

"Everyone smiles for the camera," she retorted.

Then I showed her the volcano. "Now, what's wrong with this picture?" Immediately, she went to the second line from the bottom: "I DON'T BELONG: I HATE WHO I AM, I DESPISE MYSELF." That was in the original draft.

Adamantly, she said, "No! I never felt that way. I never hated myself. I never despised myself. I was tough; I knew I was right!"

"Sorry," I quickly apologized. "I can delete that. Consider it gone." But she posed no objection to the bottom line, that others would despise her. That seemed a clue. Nor did she protest any other part of the volcano. "You know what I am doing; I'm looking for your bitter root judgment."

(A bitter root judgement is a subconscious, negative understanding of reality about oneself learned in childhood: includes self-blame, or negative self-judgement. It is a paradigm – an unrecognized pattern of thought.)

That started a verbal dance, rather a joust, as we tried to fine tune the image of the volcano, especially to get a precise and complete definition of its base. What indeed was the actual bottom line, the bitter root judgment? A number of words and phrases in various combinations were tried: fear, father figure, alone, protection, loneliness, loss of friends, chaos, psychological chaos, authority figure, co-dependency, rational proof of protection, uncontrolled environment, abandonment, stability, love associated only with the act of talking together, and probably more.

Ronda kept insisting that it was not fear of not being protected that bedeviled her excessive anxieties, but being without people who loved and understood her. Since in her family love was expressed primarily by means of constant conversation; being alone could be her feeling even surrounded by other people – alone in a crowd.

Living right near family members who do love her is not a solution because as a twin, there was a tremendously exaggerated need to be with family who totally agreed on everything, as twins usually do in early childhood. And many of Ronda's family members greatly differ with her about her most important Catholic truths.

Ronda continued, "I keep thinking, Al, that the remedy is talking constantly to Jesus, Mary and Joseph."

"That is good, Ronda, but you can't see them, can you? And you are not especially keen on e-mails or phone conversations with humans. You like to see the person you are talking with."

"Right; that's why I am so fond of Skype and go-to-meeting situations."

In spite of her protestations about protection not being the key issue, I still thought it was, so I tried to focus again on her father's abandonment of the family. Ronda agreed in part. Both she and her twin sister married father-figures, men twenty years older. And as widows both of them feel even more anxious than before those deaths.

So here is what we finally agreed. The obsessive anxiety was due to chronic codependent needs in fear and anticipation that again and again: "I am going to be rejected, abandoned and alone." This, of course, being all the more fearful as she enters her eighties. Among all her obsessive "what ifs" this keeps re-peating. As Ronda puts it, "Since for me love is conversation, what if I wind up in a convalescent home surrounded by people who can't talk much or can't talk in the way I like to communicate, and /or the ones I do like to talk to reject me? I will feel abandoned and alone."

After I suggested she had an eternal Father who never would reject her, she revealed that there was little or no anxiety when she was with, i.e., could see and talk to someone present, especially a rational, protective authority figure. "I trust the Father, but I can't see him!"

"That brings up the detachment issue, doesn't it?" I offered. "Clearly you are detached from power, wealth and the easy life – the temptations of Christ in the desert – but the most difficult is detachment from your own will." I thought she was holding back tears at that thought, that she had not really yielded all her will to the Father. She clearly was disturbed, deeply so.

"I have worked for the Lord for sixty years. Isn't that following God's will?"

"Right, I replied. "But how about God's will concerning your future life in whatever remains of it here on earth?"

"Okay," Ronda admitted. "I certainly haven't done that."

"We will keep working on that, Ronda, but for now, every time the anxiety pops up, pray the Father lead you to total trust in His will."

We ended the session there, but later that day she sent me an e-mail with these prayers for Lent:

I REBUKE THE SPIRIT OF EXCESSIVE AN-XIETY AND LAY IT AT YOUR FEET, MY JESUS; TAKE IT AWAY!

DETACH ME, LORD, FROM SCHEMING TO FILL MY NEED FOR HUMAN FATHERLY PROTECTIVE

LOVE. LET ME TRUST YOU WILL, SEND ME WHO
I NEED.

Pray as a mantra during quiet time: ABBA,
FATHER.

For Personal Reflection and Group Sharing:

- What do you think is the "bitter root" of your
excessive anxiety?"

- What way of prayer for inner healing of the
bitter root of your excessive anxiety would help
you?

Session VII

Bitter Root; Deep Waters

O God of my ancestors and Lord of mercy, who by your wisdom have formed humankind, give me the wisdom that sits by your throne, and do not reject me from among your servants.

Wisdom 9:1, 2, 4

Reject: refuse to accept, consider, hear, receive, or admit. Rebuff, repel. Parents who reject their children. To cast off. Repulse. (Webster)

<u>Spiritual Director's Introduction</u>: The last session yielded a statement of Ronda's bitter root judgment and the painful realization that she had not yielded control of her future to the will of the Father. She long since had detached from wealth, power and the easy life – the temptations of Christ – but not from her own strong will. As she put it, "I have worked for the Lord for sixty years. What do I do with *that*?"

Session six was a high-pressure consultation; had gone on for well over an hour as we searched for the right words to express her bitter root judgment. With the added issue raised regarding her will, Ronda clearly was under greater stress than I had seen before; not a prelude to anger, but a pained look of deep sorrow. I had been pretty relentless, thinking we were very close to the bitter root judgment, wanting to get it stated, NOW! Pushing too hard.

I backed off and terminated that session with the agreement that the bitter root judgement was that "Someday, I could be rejected by everyone, abandoned and alone." She decided to pray during the week for release from excessive anxiety and for trust in the Father's will for her future.

During the week, it occurred to me that our rushed statement of a bitter root judgment could not be correct. It was a present-day thought, not a judgment likely made by a child seventy odd years ago. It did not carry the seventy-year burden of all the perceived rejections, loss of trust and constant expectation of future rejections. The statement suggested current fear to me, not the root cause of fear. Perhaps "I can't trust anyone!" was a more accurate statement?

That would explain the anxiety, the anger and the search for ulterior motives she seemed to suspect of everyone. But she must speak the authentic bitter root judgement herself! It can't be my idea, accepted by her under pressure. (This session may seem confusing. I purposely wanted to explore hidden connections by way of goading Ronda into stating for herself the actual bitter root.)

+

As we started, it occurred to me that I had not made clear the two "persons" of Ronda; the visible and dynamic Ronda present across the table and the perceptions of child Ronda hidden in her sub-conscious.

I began in this way, evoking the "I can't trust anyone!" interpretation, pretty sure that she would resist. I wasn't "selling" trust as the bitter root, but urging her to resist that idea by finding her own deep-seated issue.

"Ronda, I think there is a bitter root judgment underneath the one we talked about last week. We need to distinguish between the adult Ronda and the inner child Ronda who made the bitter root judgment. The inner child yells and quakes in anger. While you, the adult Ronda, sometimes trusts, your inner child trusts no one. She does not trust face values, always looking for ulterior motives."

Ronda jumped right on that one. "For example, because of all those rejections in the past, I do look for ulterior motives. Yes, I think I do that correctly, because people do have lots of ulterior motives!"

"Not everybody, not all the time, Ronda. Maybe you think I have ulterior motives! That would be false. Do you think that, because I am working with you, I have ulterior motives?"

"Maybe, because my bad traits may be more than my good traits?! Ronda was grinning now.

I shot back, "I would work with you if you had no good traits at all, so long as you would let me. Ready to help. That's called unconditional love, isn't it?" She looked incredulous as I continued. "Actually, I think that is a woman's problem more than a man's. Women, more than men, think men have ulterior motives."

Ronda was still grinning, just less so. "Yes, but not wonderful Catholic men. Many men are motivated by lust or the desire to make a slave of a woman. That's exploitation!"

"Your bitter root is lack of trust. You can't trust anybody!" I suggested.

Ronda then revealed that her husband, she thought, had married her in part because in his earlier years he had taken care of his younger sister and she, Ronda, twenty years his junior seemed to him more like another daughter to take care of, i.e., she perceived ulterior psychological motives. She continued, "Right! I need only to trust God. I do trust God for eternal joy, but on earth I think the worst will happen since after all, even perfect Jesus was allowed by God to be crucified. So, I prayed Abba father all week and I am still anxious."

"You need to pray Abba Father from your inner child, not just your adult mind. You also need to shift from so much personal concern to affirmation of others. You already do that, just concentrate as much as possible on affirmation of others."

She responded, "I don't like the bitter root being not able to trust. It feels to me more as if the fear of being rejected and alone leads to not trusting others. Ultimately, everyone will reject me and I will be alone."

There! She finally said it!

Or, in the voice of a child, "Everyone rejects me. I am alone."

(A little child is present-focused on the moment and is most likely to speak in the present. This global judgement in the present moment of the child gets carried forward in the life of the maturing teen and adult, who is unaware of their own childhood declaration. A bitter root judgment may also be thought of as a paradigm, an unrecognized thought pattern accepted and carried forward as reality.)

Ronda continued. "Maybe I should work on an exercise where whenever I want to grab something good for my future, I just accept that God alone is enough."

"I was getting to that," I said, "You need total abandonment. Work on abandonment prayer of whatever kind you wish."

A final comment. "Abandonment" as used here actually is a reference to the virtue of detachment.

For Personal Reflection and Group Sharing:

- How do such elements as fear of rejection, the need for protection and lack of trust manifest in your anxiety?

- Can you write a prayer about these feelings?

Session VIII

Is That a Tree Limb or a Snake?

"Why are you fearful and why do you tremble when you are united to Me? I am displeased when a soul yields to vain terrors. Who will dare to touch you when you are with Me? Most dear to Me is the soul that strongly believes in My goodness and has complete trust in Me. I heap My confidence upon it and give it all it asks".

The Lord to Sr. Faustina, *Diary*, 453

<u>Spiritual Director's Introduction</u>: My intention for session VIII was to inventory what we understood in terms of Ronda's negative and positive traits, then begin to explore her need to detach from her own will in favor of the will of God for her – a trust and control issue. I will refresh the definition of detachment as we get to it. But the session developed in ways that I did not anticipate due to journal entries Ronda began to send to me in e mails between sessions.

I need to alert the reader to her conversations with Jesus. That may scandalize a few and be questioned by many others, but consider this. Our God lives; He is not above speaking with whomever He wishes, either audibly or in the heart. This spiritual director has heard His audible voice five times on four occasions; my wife journaled many conversations with Mary, mother of God, and many other serious Catholics will testify to their own experiences.

In Ronda's case, such conversations are not audible, but words "in the heart" she attributes variously to the Holy Spirit, Jesus and Mary; especially because she says they are always better than what she thinks on her own. Her journal entries are credible not only because she declares them, but because Jesus' comments were on topic! Detachment!

I first presented her with this opening list.

Ronda's inventory of negative traits

Habitual expectation of future rejections; her person, her works and her beliefs.

Habitual suspicion of ulterior motives of some others, leading to frequent anticipation of rejection or withdrawal.

Self-protection through habitual scheming about unlikely alternative perfect futures where she will be protected.

Her perception that everything is about Ronda. (This last item was new, as I had my own suspicions. It dominated the opening discussions, below.)

Ronda's inventory of positive traits

She is precious to God.

Her works are valuable, affirming and honored by her many readers despite criticism by some in her profession. They thought she should concentrate on advancement of the field of philosophy rather than on helping others through her works as a wounded healer; expressed in writings, workshops and lectures.

She is loved by those closest to her, though some actively disagree with her.

+

Ronda read over the list of traits; quietly agreed with them as factual, then questioned that new item. "What do you mean, 'Everything is about Ronda'? That's not true?! I don't think that!"

"I think you are overly self-conscious, Ronda. No, you don't think that consciously, but subconsciously you are acting that out. The best examples are those two incidents in the parking lot after Mass we've talked about several times. The car radio was on when you started to get in and you immediately thought I had turned it on so I would not have to listen to you. That radio had nothing to do with you! You were talking with Jim while standing behind the car when I turned it on. It had nothing to do with you!

"And Jim sat five rows behind us at that Mass. He explained in the car that he felt uneasy walking up to the first row after Mass had started. But you! Oh no, you immediately thought 'He sat back there because he hates to sit next to me! BS! His decision had nothing to do with you!"

Ronda was getting mildly defensive. "I don't know what you are talking about. I don't do that." "Besides, self-centeredness is unavoidable in some sense because we operate out of our own center of consciousness. I don't decide when you will go to sleep, for example."

I wanted to avoid a long philosophical discussion and stay on the topic at hand. It would be more illuminating of why Ronda is so excessively anxious. "Ronda, what makes the early teen years so difficult and painful?"

Here, I, Al, quoted Antisthenes: "The most useful piece of learning for the uses of life is to unlearn what is untrue."

She thought about the question of being overly self-conscious for a bit and then offered, "Because we think everyone is looking at us?" She had a quizzical look about her, as though she was on the verge of understanding, though still resisting the thought.

I continued, "That's part of it. Right! A teenager can think, everyone is looking at me, or talking about me, or ignoring me; they don't like me, because I am ugly or too fat, or I have double chins or whatever. I still had that problem in my freshman year at college. I was walking down the street; passed three girls going the other way. A minute later I heard them laughing though they were well past me. I was sure they were laughing at me. Their laughter I assumed to be about me!

I generalized: "We all go through that phase in the early teens. We go through various phases all our life long, even at our advanced age. The problem is, sub-consciously we can get stuck in part or all of a phase. You're stuck thinking everything you see or hear is about you and it's always negative. It's self-inflicted anxiety (!), Ronda!"

"Like the eternal child syndrome!" she exclaimed.

"Just like the eternal child! Some adults always feel as if they were little children or want to cling to that phase! I thought it was more ego-mania; Ronda the drama queen, looking to see if others will be secondary characters or cameos in my ongoing drama."

"Much like the eternal child syndrome, Ronda, only we can get stuck in part of one phase while otherwise continuing to mature physically and psychologically."

75

"What do I do about that, the eternal teen syndrome if we want to call it that?

"Now that you know about it, every time something seems to be about you – especially if it is negative - ask yourself, 'Is this really about me?' It probably isn't most of the time."

A humorous example happened once when Al was visiting my quarters to work on this book. He brought a jar of orange juice. Here is how the dialogue proceeded:

Ronda: "Do you want a glass?"

Al: "No."

Ronda: "Oh, is that because you think I don't wash my dishes well enough?"

Al: "No!!!! I was just not wanting you to have to wash another glass!"

What a perfect example of Ronda imagining everything was about her!

We concluded for the time being, but during the week, I started getting e mails relating entries from her journal. I will list them all with minimal editing, then comment.

+

March 3: It seemed Jesus said to me – You,

Ronda, are never alone because I am with you every moment. It's only that you don't open to Me, but instead cling to your own daily thoughts and actions and feelings as if I were only there when you happen to pray to Me.

Ronda: "Together Forever!" a phrase I was using about living all together with all branches of the family, seemed good as a title for this new part of my life.

I thought He added – Yes, insert your name into every liturgical prayer. Make the little chapel (in your apartment) more of a base for you, out of which you answer calls and do little deeds of love. Do you notice that you have quite a phone ministry?

How could you believe I am your bridegroom as a dedicated widow and still think you are alone? Others experience Me in the silence of their hearts, but since I have made you into a word person, it is better to talk to Me all day.

March 9: Ronda: I am upset that I had another nightmare and in the night couldn't hear Your voice in my heart any more.

Jesus – The evil spirits are angry that you are becoming nearer to Me and you must expect attacks. Keep speaking to me in your heart and trust.

Ronda: Yes, "Together, Forever," even if I cannot always hear Your "words".

March 10: Ronda: Again long sleep, but bad dreams. I woke up thinking not that You, my Jesus, will ever reject me, but that I am in for new and different interior and exterior crosses.

Jesus – Rebuke any spirit of anxiety and let me take it away. The joy of being much closer to Me will make all sufferings of these kinds bearable, as you see in those who are closer to Me.

Ronda: Oh!

+

Back to me, Al, pondering these messages.

So, what is going on here? What is this conversation between Jesus and Ronda all about? What is the unnamed subject? Detachment!

Detachment from her self-absorbed own will (the anticipation of future rejections, her scheming and dreaming up impossible futures, her assumption that all is about her) and attachment to the will and friendship of God with unconditional trust. This kind of detachment:

Detachment of will is the hardest, most necessary, and most meritorious detachment. The fully detached person leaves himself unreservedly in God's hands, "not as I will, but as thou wilt." He asks nothing and refuses nothing. From *A Catholic Dictionary*, Donald Attwater, Gen Ed.

At this point, the journal entries affirmed my thought that it was time – having discerned the sources of Ronda's difficulties – time to move ahead with a session focused on detachment. But constantly checking Ronda's progress so that we might catch a return to old habits.

Detachment needs a full discussion: it is easy to misunderstand the concept and difficult to convert from an intellectual idea of detachment to a way of life.

In closing session VIII, we recognized Ronda's progress – she seems more relaxed, her emotions are more subdued, she hasn't yelled or lectured me or shown anger in a while. We agreed that it was time to examine the concept of detachment and separately, we realized that she needed as part of her journaling, to keep track of any old habits that pop up and celebrate her ongoing victory over them.

Later that same Sunday, I got this e mail from Ronda.

PROOF OF GRACE: A therapist friend of mine I haven't talked to in 4 years spoke to me on the phone. She thought I sounded much happier and livelier!

My response? ALLELUIA!

For Personal Reflection and Group Sharing:

- What in this session reminded you of ways you sometimes think?

- What does the word detachment mean to you?

Session IX

Snake in the Boat!

As no darkness can be seen by anyone surrounded by light, so no trivialities can capture the attention of anyone who has his eyes on Christ. 'What can separate us from the love of Christ, which is in Jesus? Can affliction or distress?'

From a homily on Ecclesiastes by Saint Gregory of Nyssa

<u>Spiritual Director's Introduction</u>: Ever been alligator hunting at night in a dark, moonless cypress swamp? Ease along slow and quiet in a flat bottom John boat, the small outboard turning a slow prop near idle. You sweep the waters with a single flashlight, seeking the glint of alligator eyes. Whisper to your buddy, "Is that an alligator or a beer can?" You ease down countless winding, narrow canals. Long vines and limbs overhang narrow passages, heavily laden with algae, damp Spanish moss and broken branches. You reach up in the dark to move a dead branch or a vine out of your face. Or is that a deadly

water moccasin hanging there ready to drop into the boat? It's so hard to see! Spiritual direction can be like that!

The following description of the event occurring Thursday evening at our writers meeting where participants share chapters from the books they are writing, may seem shocking to some readers, but Ronda and I believe that you will agree after you finish the session that, as Jesus taught, "The truth will set you free."

The incident reveals the staying power of her pent-up anxiety and explosive inner-child anger which sometimes erupts. Ronda insists that before I continue, I insert her back story. Otherwise, she is afraid that the reader might think she is insane!

Ronda's back story: "For some twenty years I attended a wonderful free international group called Recovery, International; for recovery from anger, anxiety and depression. This brought me from five angry fits a day down to one a month. Still, sometimes I suddenly erupt with rage. I don't want to go into the reasons I got so angry at what I thought Al was implying, but just assure you that his description of my behavior given below is not the way I am every day!!!"

Ronda blew her stack again, this time during a meeting in her quarters of the weekly writers group she recently organized and leads at her quarters. I was discussing detachment. Once again, we were talking and thinking past each other. My illustration of the meaning of detachment happened to push her buttons.

She blew: yelling at me, furiously pounding the table; got up, pounded the furniture nearby, turned – still yelling – and collapsed back into her chair, glaring at me as would an angry little girl; she was breathing heavily, emotionally exhausted!

Certainly, I expected a relapse into the old Ronda, just didn't know when until it actually happened. Of course, shortly she apologized to the group and to me as the reality of her tantrum sank in. It was a full performance by inner-child Ronda!

Later in the meeting, she theorized that I evoked, in my role as a mentor, a father figure who seemed to belittle her opinion. Had her own father too often belittled her childhood opinions? I mention this outburst as perhaps, (we shall see), a hoped for last release; the last cry of the inner child, and as a great entre to the subject of detachment.

+

Detachment is easy to define, harder fully to understand; but necessary to incorporate as a lifetime cure of habitual anxiety. Be aware: in the following definition, the term "creatures" relates to all creation, not just animals as in common usage. Read carefully, every word is important to your understanding!

First point: "(Detachment is) an ascetic indifference to creatures, not absolute but relative to the affection had for God and divine things. True detachment consists not in a negation of affection for creatures (all of which have their part in God) but rather in an enlightened and just sense of proportion; ...

"Ronda, would you explain this first point to me?" I asked her to explain, even though I understood it, to draw her out.

"You want me to explain that to you? (Pause.) OK," Ronda began. A recently retired professor, she went right into her lecture mode.

"Detachment does not mean necessarily that we love human beings or various desires or activities less, but that we love God more. It is a question of priorities. For example, a new mother has a deep joyful love for her baby. She does not love God less, cuddling the baby with affection; but if she loves God more than the baby she won't choose to miss Sunday Mass because she rather be home with the baby. She will bring the baby to Holy Mass, even if inconvenient, rather than use the baby as a reason to skip worship of God on Sunday.

"However, choosing to love God more when there is a conflict that involves great suffering is more

difficult, e.g., to be true to God's moral commandments against adultery if someone is in a difficult
marriage, can involve much more of a struggle. When
there is a choice of God's will above human desires,
then there is a conflict."

"Difficult it can be," I agreed.

Ronda responded, "Yes, but it is not a matter of
intensity. Only mystics love God every moment of the
day and seek extreme penances and withdrawal only
into God!

Picking up on her shift of topic, I offered, "Your
comment about intense mystics pertains to extreme
cases, but not all mystics. St Benedict, for one, would
call for a balanced, prudent, objective mystic even as
does *A Catholic Dictionary* describe such under the
entry on mysticism. You, yourself know several mystics who are balanced, prudent and objective!"

I continued:

Second point: (Detachment) "is exercised in
respect of 1) material success, 2) wealth, and 3) "good
fortune," not because these things are not good in
their kind and degree but on account of their
difference in kind and relative unimportance in the
destiny of the human being considered as a whole."
That is, eternal life.

Note: in the biography of Dr. Maria Montessori.
the list from which to be detached reads "pursuit of

power, wealth, and the easy life" as she was taught in her youth by late 19th century Italian Benedictine nuns. They are the temptations of Christ in the desert. Personally, I prefer Montessori's term "easy life."

Whichever list you prefer, the issue is over excessive attachment to any aspect of creation, rather than "attachment" to the Creator. So, I related the issue to her problems with anxiety. "Ronda, the more you are attached to any of these things, the more anxiety you will feel when your possession of that person, thing, or activity is threatened in some way. So, to use an example that is not your own, an alcoholic becomes very anxious if he or she thinks that the grocery store nearby is about to close just when the beer or wine runs out."

Ronda chimed in, "Of course, that's true. So, since I am over attached to wanting to assure ideal circumstances for me in the last decade(s) of my life, I become excessively anxious when I think some plan or scheme will fall through."

We closed the session on that note.

+

There are other ways to understand Ronda's issues, as well: Myers-Briggs Psychological Topology gives a clear statement of the problem. This analysis may seem unrelated, but read carefully and you will see how eventually, it helps to explain Ronda's excessive anxiety.

According to this topology, there are sixteen basic psychological types which can be described as variations of four pairs of psychological traits. The four pairs are:

(E) EXTROVERT   or perhaps rather   (I)
    INTROVERT

(N) INTUITIVE   or perhaps rather   (S)
    SENSATE

(T) THINKING   or perhaps rather   (F)
    FEELING

(J) JUDGING   or perhaps rather   (P)
    PERCEIVING

A necessary distinction: most people are primarily one or the other of these polarities, but not exclusively

FIRST PAIR: Some people gain energy from being with people (extrovert); others gain energy being alone (introvert).

SECOND PAIR: Some persons perceive the world in a more abstract manner (intuitive); others perceive the world in a more concrete sensory manner).

THIRD PAIR: Some persons prefer to make their decisions based in their thought about an issue (thinking), others prefer to decide based on emotions (feeling).

FOURTH PAIR: Some persons prefer to act on what they perceive as orderly (judging); others prefer flexibility, playing it by ear (perception).

As an example, Ronda tests closely in this way:

1) She is a strong <u>extrovert</u> (E); i.e., she gains energy with people, loses energy working alone. She gets anxious when alone.

2) She is an extremely <u>intuitive</u> abstract perceiver of reality (N); i.e., perceives reality through ideas rather than in the concrete. That makes her a good philosopher, but you would not want her to try to fix the plumbing. She gets extremely anxious about any physical task like driving, turning a lock, using technology equipment, etc.

3) She is closely balanced between <u>thinking</u> (T) and <u>feeling</u> (F); i.e., makes decisions either by thinking or feeling and

4) She has a strong preference for orderliness as in punctuality, written schedules, etc., and sometimes lacks flexibility. (J) She gets anxious when things are not orderly.

Each type has strengths and weaknesses. Ronda's strengths are obvious. So are her weaknesses. Balanced between thinking and feeling she suffers the weaknesses of both. For example, on the thinking side, over-analysis of other people's statements. And, on the feeling side, emotional reactions that are inappropriate.

Here is the point! Since Ronda's preference for decision making by thinking or feeling are so well balanced, she is prone to the faults of both. Combined with a difficult upbringing and marriage, it is no wonder she is struggling with cynical attitudes, ridged classification of people, feelings of rejection, anxiety and anger.

For Personal Reflection and Group Sharing:

- Did you identify with Ronda's explosion of anger? If so were there any insights of Al helpful?

- About psychological topology. If you are familiar with Myers-Briggs, how would you describe yourself? If not, reading such a short analysis, do you see any relationship between your anxiety problems and the topology you think fits you?

Interlude

Open Waters!
Where are We?

*Could anything remain hidden in me? I would only
be hiding you from myself. I am displeased with
myself. I have renounced myself and chosen you,
recognizing that I can please neither you nor myself
unless you enable me to do so.*

From the *Confessions* of Saint Augustine

Ronda is a warrior; acceptably so in her professional realm as a meritorious professor of philosophical
truth. Her appropriate adversaries are other philoso-
phers with whom she disagrees. But her most difficult,
unyielding adversary is her inner child. She constantly
is in an uneasy stalemate with herself, often breaking
into out of control warfare at the slightest hint of
opposition.

What, so far have we learned?

In our spiritual direction sessions, we first tracked down the bitter root judgment: her subconscious belief that she will be despised and rejected by everyone, sooner or later she will be alone. Her anxiety is a constant anticipation of another rejection. Not surprising as the long-term effect of her father's seeming verbal rejection of her childhood verbal conversational gambits. Further, his abandonment at a critical age, just after she reached the age of reason. A young girl most needs a good relationship with her father around this time.

Ronda's father announced his departure from her mother to marry another woman and live with her and this woman's teenage daughter. He then left the twin eight year old girls to walk back home alone, standing on a west side New York street as he walked away. Afterwards, they would see him only on Sunday visits.

This disaster was made all the worse by the natural weaknesses of Ronda's place in psychological topology. Her tendencies are expressed in critical, cynical attitudes; classifying people rigidly, getting caught up in a system of thought that she tries to sell; experiencing frequent fear of being alone and chronic expectation of being rejected!

If that is not enough, we discovered she sometimes relates everything she sees and hears from others as a sign of rejection (normative only for the early teen years). When she does lose control, she uses the weapons of the angry, terrible two-year old! Some people do get partially stuck in early developmental phases. When Ronda loses control, she strikes out as expected of a two-year old! Her inner child delivers a hair trigger explosion of outrage!

So what is the good news? The good news is that Ronda is beginning to get it. In fits (pun intended) and starts, her combat has become with anxiety, itself. A few examples from her work, her journal and our sessions will suffice.

Several weeks past, she was invited to give a parish Lenten mission. She was elated that a lay person, *and a woman(!),* was asked to give a mission. That is almost unheard of. Yet, a pastor who had never met her, heard or knew much of her credentials and many workshop successes invited her on the basis of having read her autobiography: *En Route to Eternity.*

Here are excerpts from Ronda's journal regarding the beginning of the mission. "I was in a situation where (the priest) seemed to be rejecting me in a surprising way, concerning an area where I am much acclaimed. I was rehearsing angry, sarcastic retorts. But there was a charismatic spiritual warrior at the same event. She prayed over me immediately and suggested that I ask the Holy Spirit how to respond; to offer up the pain of the encounter for the priest.

"Instead of doing the drama queen scenario, I went

sort of numb and at the next encounter...allowed the Holy Spirit to take over with very positive results all around. I believe that being more aware of my fear of rejection helped me to see that my anger was a compensation for that fear. I was able to deal better with this situation than I would have before."

After the first evening talk of the mission, Ronda called me in desperation. The pastor had criticized her opening performance.

"What did the priest say," I asked Ronda.

"He said I was being too academic; needed to spice it up with personal anecdotes, etc. She wailed to me, "I've been doing this for fifty years! I know what works!" Fear of rejection was fully engaged.

Close by her in the background, I could hear two women talking, seeming to advise her though I could not hear distinctly. I inquired. They were two friends. "They are telling me to thank him!" Ronda complained, "To tell him I will pray about it, and will do what I can!"

"They are on scene," I said, "and I am halfway across the country. What they say sounds perfectly reasonable. I am not going to advise you except to say, do what they say."

The next day she called me, rejoicing! The second talk of the mission was given with an audience of 100. The priest sat in the back row in clear view of Ronda.

She could see him clearly, sitting as though judge and jury.

At the end of her presentation – she did spice it up with numerous personal anecdotes – he rushed up exclaiming, "Ronda! That was a home run! You knocked it out of the park!"

"He was right!" she exclaimed. (About spicing it up.)

Point being, with a little help she stayed out of warrior mode, deferred to the priest, and won the battle with kind humility rather than certainly losing in conflict. She came home triumphant!

After the Mission, Ronda met with her old friend, Alice Von Hildebrand, now 94! Alice is equally famous, perhaps more so than Ronda, in Catholic philosophical circles.

(From Ronda's journal), "Alice said, 'The reason we hate ourselves is because we cannot adore ourselves!' She meant that out of pride we want to admire ourselves as perfect and since we are not perfect we despise ourselves. Instead, we need humbly to rely on God's mercy. Alice also talked to Ronda about femininity and receptivity. Very gently she said, 'You, Ronda, could have more of that.' This fits with Al's contention that I want too much to be perfect. Receptivity could be very good for me vs. pushy, anxious project-i-tis!"

Thus ends the mission account. But here are two more journal entries.

"(Another) friend says I am imperfect in my defects and God loves me just the way I am. Not that God loves my sins, but that He doesn't despise me for being a sinner. I made an act of accepting God's permissive will for the rest of my life.... When I mentioned this to Al he said that I must be sure this is not just in my head, but also in my heart.

"At dinner with friends of Al, I was talking about my symptom of nail picking. I told them that I am much worse when I am sitting near Al. Why would that be? One of them said 'It is the white coat syndrome. It is proven that our blood pressure goes up as soon as we see the doctor!"

There are other events, but the above gets the point across. There is change ongoing in Ronda's life, in fits (!) and starts, but actually.

+

Ronda writes this in her journal, before the birthday party she and her twin celebrated on their 80th. (Ronda, her twin sister Carla, daughter Diana and friend Paula prepared for the feast and frivolity.) "I was up in the night overly anxious about the birthday weekend coming up. Jesus seemed to tell me, 'Holy Saturday was terrible for the Apostles. They only had the faintest hope and much horror from the crucifixion. So, since you want to be a disciple vs. a customer, I allowed you a taste of the very minor uncertainty about the visit for the birthday.'

(This contrast between the customer and the disciple comes from the writings of Richard Wurmbrand. He asks us as Christians whether we just want to be customers, that is people who want good things from God in answer to their prayers, or disciples, that is, those who want to be like Jesus, suffering the way He did.)

Jesus continued, 'But expect big joys and graces on this 80th birthday coming not from you, but from the others to you.' Right after that came good things in the family."

I, Al, was at the party. It was joyous! But what happened in the hour before the party needs telling. I was asked to present a short prayer service just for Ronda and another family member. The hope was for reconciliation in avoidance of old familial conflicts that could erupt during the party.

Let me paint a mental image of the two.

We sat in a very small room, the prayer room of the quarters where Ronda resides. I, seated, faced the two; they were seated half facing each other, both facing me. The other was more or less relaxed and passive, receptive, but Ronda sat stiff and erect, stern of face, as though prepared for conflict. She reminded me of an owl or hawk on a limb, ready to swoop down and capture a gentle victim. Keep this picture in mind as you read the exhortation which I composed and read aloud to them during the prayer service.

+

Exhortation

It begins with the terrible two's: very young, a child just has discovered she is not an extension of her mother; she is an individual! Echoing the great I AM whence she came, the child discovers, "I am!" She never again will feel so free!

This new and exciting discovery has to be explored; "I am free!" There seem to be no boundaries. "What can I not do? How far is there to go?" And all too soon, "What can I get? What can I control?"

The terrible two begins without prudence, without humility, without charity, without mercy. The personhood of others yet is not learned. And that other child is an object that might be controlled. Grasping for control begins.

The child has means: yelling, threatening, insulting, ridiculing, hitting, teasing, cajoling, rejecting, crying, tantrums; orchestrated as necessary to get one's way. Children are subjected, and they subject others, to such behavior.

Something else is happening out of sight. The

developing mind buries away thought patterns, behavioral patterns and false assumptions about reality. Juvenile ideas and conflicts are laid quietly in shallow graves.

Older now, we are students of life, we sublimate controlling behavior. Yet the child is not dead, she lives; old conflicts in shallow graves arise, awaiting opportunity to declare once again, "I am!" Beware!

The inner child often re-appears in family gatherings; old conflicts renew in old familial contexts. Controlling habits arise once more. Rather, detach from prideful control and self-will; listen to the Lord who speaks. "Love one another, as I have loved you."

+

I fully expected a quiet, sedate, traditional prayer meeting. That is not what I got. Immediately, it turned into a free-wheeling session of double spiritual direction. In general, the other was both gently expressive and receptive. But Ronda the philosopher, slightly receptive, was impulsively overriding; she countered or restated much that the other tried to express.

As it turned out, Ronda was controlling. She had to be right and she had to be heard in her desire for perfect expression of every issue that came up.

Of course, I pointed this out. In process, that lit

Ronda's fuse, as I reminding them of St. Paul's exhortation, "Defer to one another."

To her credit, Ronda did not blow. But she was unhappy, temporarily defiant. She interpreted deference as deferring from the truth, and that was not her philosophical game! But deferring to one another is merely an act of courtesy, of hearing the other person out, of recognizing the integrity and right of another to speak, i.e., an act of unconditional love. Indeed, with intense discussion we did get past that speed bump. Afterward, Ronda insisted I include the above exhortation for your benefit.

I should add that just before the closing psalm, I gave them a ten-minute interlude to speak to one another in private. Do not know what they said to one another, don't want to know; but the party was an uproarious success.

The question now, is this. Our Sunday sessions of spiritual direction were interrupted for several weeks; by the Lenten mission, by Holy Week and the Easter Vigil, by the party. The issue of detachment was raised before the interruption. I have no doubt that Ronda adequately has been spiritually detached from creation for many years; but is she ready for the test? The most difficult will be her detachment from her own strong will. She tends habitually to dominate. To impose her will or beliefs on others and to try to get her will in all situations, even when the choice is between two goods. Detachment from one's own will is the door to life without anxiety of any sort. Is she ready?

From the beginning, it has been two steps forward, one step back; a slow dance always resulting in a little progress. Ever try to walk up a sand dune? At every step up, you sift and slide nearly back to where you were. Surely, she will slip and slide back. She is fighting habits of a life time. But, yes. She is tired of being tired. She would be done with anxiety. She is tough. She will make it happen.

On to the test. Two steps forward, one step back. By the Grace of God. Selah.

For Personal Reflection and Group Sharing

- After reading this interlude about Ronda's journey, so far, how do you feel about your own journey from anxiety along the road to spiritual joy?

Session X

Castle of the Swamp Queen

Peace be within your walls, and security within your towers. For the sake of my relatives and my friends I will say, "Peace be within you. For the sake of the house of the Lord our God, I will seek your good.

Psalm 124: 7

The first nine sessions were worked in a dark, foggy swamp. Ronda's alligators could be sensed in passing; a ripple, a muffled splash, something slightly defined moving in the shallows. Just before dawn we caught sight of her; "Rejection", the mother of all alligators. Then her children, "Control" and "It's All About Me" and "Perfection" and "Anger" and "Rage". Ronda rules as judge of truth; restating, correcting, refuting much that others say. Unmistakable! Ronda controls. To deny her is to risk rage.

Ronda defends the castle of perfect truth and exposition. Alligators swim in her moat, the drawbridge and gates are closed. Ronda is secure. From the highest tower, under pennants of truth and perfect exposition, she proclaims her word in writings and workshops. All is well for those who adore. Those weak of truth or divergent in exposition are rewarded with immediate correction.

Should anyone dare confront, the drawbridge drops, the gates swing open and out comes – not the Ronda we know and love, but – Samurai Chervin! She slashes with the two-edge sword of truth and rages with the armor breaking mace of obedience until her enemies are subdued. All but the strongest offender retreat and fall back.

Samurai Chervin perceives retreat as rejection; returns to her castle, draws up the bridge, closes the gates and feasts on renewed anxiety. I pointed this out more gently in an early session, saying "Ronda, you are causing your own anxiety." The most important act of receptivity Ronda can make is to be receptive of God's will; i.e., detach from her own! To be receptive of God's permissive will *and* the personhood of others. She needs actively to recognize that the personhood of others includes their freedom to disagree with her even when she is sure she is right. It's that simple and that difficult. Ronda knows this. But:

To know and not to do, is not yet to know.

Ronda's transformation could begin easily; just by

being nice; receptive of others who seem to question or propose alternative ideas. Pleasantly, to acknowledge the expression of others, even God's own permissive expression. By all means, continue to swing the two edged sword of truth; she offers much good from her life and studies. Many acknowledge her truths now and others will follow. But leave the mace in the castle!

These are the sacrifices most pleasing to God: mercy, humility, praise, peace, charity. Such as these, then, let us bring and free from fear, we shall await the coming of the Judge who will judge the world in equity... the peoples in his truth. (St. Augustine)

Samurai Chervin is strong, she can do this; she will do this when she decides.

+

To some, the characterization of Samurai Chervin will seem brutal. (I prefer "blunt"). Those who know her will be laughing or shaking their heads in acknowledgment of its brash metaphoric accuracy. When Ronda read this during a manuscript editing session, she lowered her head dismally. I thought that was tough on her. I need to be affirming with her in process.

What did Ronda think? To her credit she acknowledged accuracy of my diagnosis. For her it was a look in the mirror.

As we arrived in the parking lot for Mass that Sunday, she gave me a mock chastisement with a big grin on her face.

"You know, Al, after reading your account of my awful controlling mechanisms, I finally have figured out your whole strategy as a spiritual director:

1) Shower the directee with affirming praise. (Just before I retired to Corpus Christi, Texas, Al wrote a welcoming letter describing the joys he and all our mutual friends would have with the arrival of Ronda).

2) Surround the directee with kindness. This will lower any defenses that a person might have. (Al generously offered me rides to Mass, brunches at his expense, etc.)

3) Encircle the directee, throwing out clues to what may be the bitter root problem. (Everything described in our early sessions).

4) Thrust the two-edged sword of truth into the directee's heart. (The analyses in the last few sessions and especially the samurai metaphor.)

5) Pray that, after these stabs, the directee, with God's grace, will resurrect and start more surely on the road to spiritual joy. (I, Al, might add, "Rather than run away from the revelation.").

She also remarked that the devil has the same

strategy, giving us seeming gifts if we fall into the temptations he offers, then letting us die in our sins, except that he offers no resurrection, only despair!

Not bad! I stand convicted of my general strategy. But, of course, the details vary widely from one directee to another.

So what was her written response to my analysis of her character? A seven point lament over Samurai Chervin and indirectly a program for healing. We discussed it point by point during the Sunday session, but her lament and implied program speaks for itself. No further dialog need be reported. We are agreed, the next step in her healing is the necessary detachment from her powerful self-will. Here is her seven-point response to the Samurai Chervin metaphor, her lament and implied program.

"I went into prayer and these are my thoughts.

1) Horror at the picture of my rejecting anyone who doesn't adore me.

2) Desire to flee into total silence and leave the world!

3) I challenged Al; he couldn't mean that all those who do have God's truth should just accept error and sin with bland passivity. What about the prophets? Al replied that just the same, since God permits others to err and sin, we can't just try to force truth into them.

4) In prayer, Jesus seemed to say, "It wouldn't be bad for you to become much more silent, at least for a time! I have drawn you into this place where I can heal you more of anger and anxiety. Open to what is true in Al's description."

5) Accepting God's permissive will in the freedom of others to err and sin would lead to speaking the truth with love vs. hateful anger and rejection of them. This would include even tiny conflicts since these also show trying to control others.

6) I can't do it...only God can draw me into His heart to have such hope of spiritual joy in heaven that I can accept the suffering of not being able to control anything or anyone on earth. Making an angry scene involves wanting to have a symbolic victory over the others. Speaking the truth with love gives the possibility of win/win vs. lose/lose. Jesus tells me that "Victory is Mine." It comes only at the end of the world, not in my encounters with others

7) Let go, let God. I am thinking of how Jesus told me long ago that if I trusted in Him I would never worry about anything again for the rest of my life."

May I, Al, add, "Amen!" May I also add by contra-distinction that underneath the issue of Ronda's excessive need to control is the antidote of authentic humility. *He who humbles himself will be exalted.* (Lk 18: 9-14.)

Humility often is presented as a character weakness, but weakness of character is not humility; it is simply weakness of character. Often, the authentically humble person is the truly strong one in the room. Humility is not about weakness vs. power or control, but about truth. It is...

An appreciation and external expression of (a person's) true position with respect to God and his neighbor; opposed therefore, both to pride and to immoderate self-abjection. (It) is an absolutely necessary prerequisite and the first of the virtues to the extent that it removes the greater obstacles to faith, upon which all rests. (A Catholic Dictionary, Donald Attwater, ed.)

For Ronda and for any other obsessively controlling person, the controlling personality actually is expressing a sometimes fatal weakness; the inability to perceive intellectual or actionable truth beyond his own view of particular situations. Opposites of humility include arrogance, personal pride beyond truth, self-importance beyond truth, etc.

In short, humility is truth about our place relative to others and especially relative to the transcendent God. To continue with the definition of humility,

...affected humility is odious and the virtue does

not require that a man should deprecate his ability...(but) consists in keeping oneself within one's own bounds, ...neither narrower nor wider than they really are.

Or as earlier suggested, Ronda should continue to swing the two-edged sword of truth, but leave the mace in the castle.

For Personal Reflection and Group Sharing

- Has anyone ever told it to you like it is with you? This Spiritual Director told Ronda, "Even if you thought that your "accuser" was cruel or mistaken in some way, what were the truths in his/her analysis of your character?

Session XI

Son Rise Over the Swamp

"Satan can even clothe himself in a cloak of humility, but he does not know how to wear the cloak of obedience."

St. Faustina's Diary

<u>Spiritual Director's Introduction</u>: Ronda continues to struggle with release of her will to control in favor of the will of God who is all in all. Final victory for her may be a day, a week, a month, a year away; <u>attained when habitually she gracefully accepts and works with the good, the bad and the ugly in every passing moment</u>. Such is the nature of detachment. But first, we need to be clear regarding God's will. What is it that we must obey to banish obsessive anxiety?

God's will is classified in two parts, "expressed" (also called "perfect") and "permissive." Think of it, also, as "general" and "personal", i.e., His will for everyone and his will for you alone.

God's expressed, general will: His will for all of us is expressed in Christian Scripture, *The Catechism of the Catholic Church*, and the teachings of the Catholic Magisterium as promulgated by faithful Catholic priests. One fully appreciates the value of these teachings by living an active, sacramental life within the Church.

God's expressed, personal will: Many practicing Christians discover through prayer, discernment and simple observation that God offers individual guidance. Christian libraries are full of books on the subject of prayer and discernment. By way of quick explanation...

> *All of us are interested in what Heaven may think...so most of us are interested in "signs". We get them in many ways...through what we read...through what others say... through what we see. "God speaks quietly, but He gives us all kinds of signs. In retrospect, especially, we can see that He has given us a little nudge through a friend, through a book, or through what we see as failure---even through accidents. If we remain alert, then slowly they piece together a consistent whole, and we begin to feel how God is guiding us".*

Pope Benedict XVI

God's permissive will: Good things happen to bad people, bad things happen to good people; often we do not see our plans (our will) fulfilled. Hurricanes and wars happen. Pain and suffering and disappoints are part of life. Why? It's about the physical laws of nature and free will. Physical laws of nature keep order in the universe. God will not destroy the order of his own creation, returning to chaos.

Free will defines us as human *in the likeness of God*. Other folks also have a separate free will with conflicting ideas, understandings and goals. God will not negate His own glory. *The Glory of God is man, fully alive.* (Irenaus.)

The natural order and our free will perdure. "Man proposes, God disposes", a homey way of acknowledging permissive will. Detachment of will includes gracious, even willing acceptance of all that actually happens in our lives; considered to be the permissive will of God. Whatever actually happens - regardless of our desires - is allowed by God.

Here is another homey observation and thought by example: while you, in a hurry, sit fuming at a red light, consider that if you had made the previous green light, you may have caused or been in an accident just ahead. We cannot know what disasters we might encounter if we got our way!

And so, prudence leads us to detachment from our will in favor of God's will.

Detachment of will: An ascetic indifference to one's own will. Detachment of will is the hardest..., most meritorious detachment. The fully detached person leaves himself unreservedly in God's hands, "not as I will, but as thou wilt." A Catholic Dictionary, (Donald Attwater, Gen Ed.)

The word "ascetic" refers to rigorous self-discipline; as used here a practiced, disciplined yielding of one's own will to the will of God. Keep fixed in mind that you *do not negate* your own will (that is not possible), but yield to God's own will *if it differs from yours.*

+

Since her miraculous conversion at 21, Ronda has built her life upon acceding to the expressed will of God, committed and searching for truth. But has battled throughout her life against God's permissive will in this guise; she brooks no opposition. Not so much by intent, but by manner. We know why. Unbidden, her alligators rise up out of the dismal swamp of a dysfunctional upbringing: mother "Rejection" and all her little ones, "Control", "It's All About Me", "Perfection", "Anger", and "Rage". Still, elimination of Ronda's anxiety is just one step away. A state of continual spiritual joy is just two steps away.

Ronda continues to struggle with final acceptance of God's permissive will; has to overcome lifetime habitual overreactions to the opposition of others. The battle will be won when she habitually responds to opposition in word or deed with loving, gentle responses; tells her truth gently and encouragingly, then accepts the freedom of others in their expression, response and belief. When she accomplishes this, she will learn to yield to the will of God. In effect, there will be nothing left to be anxious about! She will be at peace.

The following are selected journal accounts of her ongoing battle.

May 1: Ronda: I am pondering the acceptance of difference, conflict, jabs of verbal persecution.

[From now on I will not add a phrase such as "Jesus seemed to say..." but just say "Jesus". We have made clear previously these are Ronda's in-the-heart perceptions.]

I perceive that I am dealt with by superior powers. This is a pleasure, a joy, an existence which I have not procured myself. I speak as a witness on the stand, and tell what I have perceived. (Thoreau)

Jesus - You want a tidy solution to all the problems of your life, the Church and the world. That only will be, in a deeper way, at the Last Judgement. For now, you have to bear the cross of all the unresolved problems, but bear it with me. You dream of leaving the world in what you would call cold anger of withdrawal. I want you to love your "enemies" –

that is, all who will not obey your truths, advice or even tiny directives.

Ronda: Jesus, help me to forgive _____ and _____ and _____ and _____ for not agreeing with the truth as I see it, for not following my advice, or my daily directives.

Jesus - Is your fear that error and sin finally will win? When that fear emerges from the depth of your soul, rush into my mind, my heart, My soul.

Ronda: Worst case is that the Church splits in two. That is a legitimate concern. Since I live so simply, I easily can move to wherever the true Church continues. What I shouldn't do is cover the fear of the "other side" winning with rage expressed as the desire to see the enemy destroyed. The spiritual joy is that "nothing can separate me from you, my Jesus".

Ronda: Later in the day I had a glitch with something in a manuscript I was editing involving a former Catholic's slur on the Church. I got anxious about asking the author to clarify the comment. Instead of getting excessively anxious and angry, I got the impulse to call the author on the phone; who readily agreed to my clarification. Win-win!

May 2. Ronda: I woke up rattled by a nightmare involving losing my purse in some large institution. I started to get anxious, wondering if it was some kind of sign that I have to save more money. When I mentioned the issue to Jesus He seemed to say:

Jesus - Never act out of anxiety. Bring the spirit of excessive anxiety to me to take away. The concern you should bring to me in quiet prayer, when first you have let Me bring you into a place of inner peace and trust.

Al: Ronda mentioned the nightmare to me later, in person. I pointed out that according to dream interpretation, dreams speak to us in symbols. Just as in a man's dream an automobile usually is a symbol of the self, so the purse could be a symbol of herself, lost in the world as she has known it. A subconscious reaction to disorientation.

Ronda: Surprise of good response from Fr. F_____ to my plan for parish talks. Surprise of the M_____'s for wanting me to do creative teaching with their children. Very good talk with G_____. He is being so expressive of love and admiration for my work. I am touched.

Note to the reader: In Ronda's previous entry, notice the expectation of rejection?

Jesus - I want you (Ronda) to die like the grain of wheat in the Gospels. I don't want you to waste any energy on hate. I want you truly to become an instrument of my love in the world.

Ronda: A thought; basically, I never have accepted the way the fallen world is, as allowed by God's permissive will. In this instance, that the "miracle" of tech is accompanied by whatever glitches have not yet been improved. I have to come to each situation balancing the joy of seeing the live faces of my loved ones with the frustrations of static, difficulty of getting on, etc. (Go to Meeting family prayer group on Internet.)

Al: We all need to listen to Gamaliel (who advised Jewish religious authorities against the crucifixion of Jesus), telling the Sanhedrin not to interfere with the man from Galilee. If he is a fraud, his movement will die of its own weight. If he is who he says he is, you may be fighting God, Himself!

The same is true with things that happen against our will. If you are fighting with God's permissive will, guess who loses?! Mistakes and bad happenings are necessary to free will.

Things do happen that we can make right. God likely will permit us to make it right. But much happens that we can do nothing about. The lesson? If you can "fix it", do so. If you can't, let it go. It is not worth the energy loss of anxiety. Pick your battles carefully, Samurai!

Ronda: I woke up (from an afternoon nap) feeling light and joyful. I remembered Jesus at another time saying that He weans us from this world by our sorrows, but gives us foretaste of heaven in our joys.

I got a PR call from Marriott about possibly winning a cruise. I yelled into the phone that I am an 80 year old woman and I don't go on cruises!!! Afterwards, I thought about it in terms of God's permissive will, and got the helpful thought that (such calls are) a part of capitalism that has led to many benefits for mankind. I should just calm down and except it. I could have said that on the phone without rage! Smile.

When talking to G_____, he talked about a personality typology in a way that I have always argued with him about. I started to raise my voice, but then stopped – thinking about the Samurai image. As a result, I got to know personal reasons why he dislikes typologies so much, which helped me to understand this dear friend better.

May 3. Ronda: I just read in de Caussade's *Abandonment to Divine Providence* about how God sanctifies through acceptance of His perfect (expressed) and permissive will, not by us speculating about it. This is exactly what you are trying to get me to see, Al – that by talking about it too philosophically, I am being defensive!

Al: It is true that if you are fully detached, you accept moment to moment reality as it is, not as you wish it to be. That is in the immediate moment to moment term. However, in the longer term, some situations you can improve upon and it is your duty to improve on reality to the extent you can, but not by force. God does not force, you shouldn't. Forcing another is lose/lose in the long term. Your anger and rage reject others and prevent their acceptance of your truths!

If reality overrides your efforts, willingly, graciously accept God's permissive will. State your truth calmly and forthrightly, listen to your opponent graciously, make your point in peace and move on; like Jesus on the paths and byways of Palestine. Again, as you previously recognized somewhere, acceptance is win/win in the long run. Peace usually is more effective in the long run. Samurai, pick your battles carefully.

Often, someone will oppose you, not because he understands you and disagrees, but because his habit and approach to life *always is* to win arguments, not seek truth. If you remain at peace, he will think he has won, perhaps think later about what you said, and agree with you in some measure. If not, it is his problem, not yours. Ronda received this quote the same day from a friend.

When the soul wraps itself around the things and the people of this world, looking for satisfaction or fulfillment that only God can give, it produces a distortion in itself, and in others as well. Many spiritual writers call the process of unwinding this possessive, self-centered clinging and disordered seeking of things and persons, "detachment." The goal of the process of detachment is not to stop loving the things and people of this world, but quite the contrary, to love them even more truly in God, under the reign of Christ, in the power of the Holy Spirit. Things and people become even more beautiful and delightful when we see them in this light.

There are almost always painful dimensions to this process of "letting go" in order to love more, but it's the pain of true healing and liberation. Christian detachment is an important part of the process by which we enter into a realm of great freedom and joy. (Ralph Martin)

May 7. Ronda: A four day visit by L_____ and M_____ to work on their book. I think I did much better, not trying to control everything; noticing when that impulse started to come into play, I stopped and offered up my annoyances.

+

Al: When an alligator is uncertain or senses a prey, he sinks a little deeper into the muddy water 'till only his eyes are there, protruding above his head. That is all you get. Two eyes watching. Ronda's alligators are like that. They have been threatened, but they are still there.

This is progress! She may relapse more than once, but that should not surprise anyone. She is battling habits of as much as 70 years! More than once, I have seen in her face anger or frustration start to rise, only to see her beat it back. You can sense that in the journal, above, and I see it directly.

At the end of his quote, Ralph Martin hints at joy to come. It will come. Don't know when, but I am confident. There is only one more step to sustained spiritual joy beyond authentic, full detachment!

For Personal Reflection and Group Sharing

- How well do you accept God's permissive will in your daily life in such situations as bad drivers, bad weather, difficult or rebellious adult children, etc.

Session XII

Customs of the Swamp Dwellers

The principle effect of the power of custom is to seize and ensnare us in such a way that it is hardly within our power to get ourselves back out of its grasp and return unto ourselves to reflect and reason about its ordinances…. And the common notions that we find in credit around us and infused into our soul by our fathers' seed, these seem to be universal and natural ones. Whence it comes to pass that what is off the hinges of custom, people believe to be off the hinges of reason….

Montaigne

Montaigne is speaking of paradigms; the entrenched habits or patterns of thought resident in our subconscious, learned from cultural assumptions of "our fathers", the secular culture. Paradigmatic habits impose subconscious boundaries on our thinking;

boundaries which often are not real. Ideas which fall outside the boundaries are rejected without recognition or consideration. Secular culture would teach that to detach from desire for power, wealth, the easy life, and personal control is against all reason.

Ronda now is in a fight against obsessive personal control, the secularly approved custom of attempting control of all aspects of her life and environment. It indeed is an internal battle against her difficult past in search of a more joyous future.

John the Baptist, speaking of Jesus is quoted saying "He must increase, while I must decrease." But Ronda is not Herod and I am not John. Hopefully she won't take my head off during her fight! Her struggles are instructive, so we will increase our attention to her journaling, though I may not decrease my commentary.

She knows what is needed, accepts the insights gained over the last four months at least intellectually, yet struggles. Her alligators and seventy year habits are not going to give up without a fight! As we proceed, pay attention to the combatants: hope and change vs. fear and regress. We return to her journal.

May 10. Ronda: Horrible nightmare (last night): I am at some Catholic conference in a large building. I don't know the people. I suddenly remember that I am supposed to meet Al at a certain time right nearby. When I get there, he is furious because I forgot him.

His face is full of disappointment and anger. He turns on his heels and walks away. I run after him, and when he faces me he still is angry.

I explain that I have to go back to the conference because a Bishop is saying the Mass. I run back to the institution, but I realize when I get there that I know no one and they are on the "other side" of the Church (dissenting, not magisterial). I wake up hurt, rejected, and frantically anxious.

I realize it was a nightmare, I rebuke the spirit of excessive anxiety; but the feeling lingers of rejection. I theorize that I am unconsciously linking Al to my father....

Spiritual Director's commentary: Suspected linking to her father has come up before.

Ronda: I try to accept that in God's permissive will, He allowed me to have this nightmare just when I was thinking I was healed by Him through Al. I decided not to call Al as a way of proving to myself that having a nightmare is not a reason to need reassurance.

Spiritual Director's commentary: My first impression was that the nightmare was an extension of the previous "lost purse" dream scenario from several days previously. I wrote back, "Your interior world is challenged, with a great deal of subconscious uncertainty and disorientation. Stay the course. You are losing your old self (the purse was symbolic of self). If

I seemed angry and accusing in the latest nightmare, it is because I really am challenging the old Ronda with a new way of understanding the dynamics of life.

But I missed two other interpretations of note. The dream could be a replay of her father abandoning her on a New York City street; with the shock and fear that abandonment would cause an eight-year old, returning to a family home that no longer was the same without a father in it.

Or, even a projection onto me of her own defense mechanism of anger? People have all kinds of defense mechanisms: anger, physical violence, passive aggressive behavior, selective listening, "forgetting", refusal to discuss certain issues, intentional misunderstanding, pretense of superior knowledge, physical avoidance, etc.

And of course, two or all three interpretations may be intertwined. The lesson of the nightmare being revelation of her internal conflict. Now to continue with her journal.

May 11: Ronda: All night wondering about a huge change concerning my future. It involved a temptation against my private promise as a Dedicated Widow. In the morning I got this response from Jesus.

Jesus - I want you to feel loved and protected by myself and by others close to you.

Ronda: Please give me a sign when I open the

Liturgy of the Hours. I opened to Psalm 16 and got "Oh Lord, it is you who are my portion and cup; it is you yourself who are my prize. The lot marked out for me is my delight: welcome indeed the heritage that falls to me! I will bless the Lord who gives me counsel, who even at night directs my heart...You will show me the path of life, the fullness of joy in your presence, at your righthand happiness forever."

That seems very clear that you want me for yourself. It seems as if that is your perfect will, but your permissive will could include other options.

After talking to Al about the above I got the sense I have to totally stop speculating about the future and thankfully receive all the love that is given me day by day from Jesus and all those around me.

I took a nap and woke up with a long "rapture" – a foretaste on the road to spiritual joy?

May 12: Ronda: I awoke filled with joyful rapture again...also with a sense of Al's wounded healer kindness in what I could have felt as rejection by him....

Jesus - I give my beloved consecrated disciples moments of spiritual joy as foretastes of heaven and encouragement on the dusty road.

Spiritual Director's Commentary: In Ronda's view, that nightmare reported on the May 10 entry was about fear of rejection. An upwelling of her life long fear, the mother of all her alligators. It was an unguarded relapse let loose in a state of sleep. But what did she mean by "wounded healer?"

I received that same morning from Ronda, the following e mail beginning with a comment similar to her journal entry just above. "I woke up this morning, again bathed in joy. Thank you for your insights and prayers. When you write about your feelings of rejection as a child, (you should) write that the wounded healer comes in when you go overboard affirming others, not to let other people feel rejected by you, especially when they might think they are being rejected by you in some form!" She refers to both an issue and a concept. The issue is a reference to my own childhood.

When it first became clear that expectation of rejection was Ronda's bitter root judgment, her mother of all alligators, I shared with her my experience of rejection by my own father. This came up in conversations with Ronda a number of times.

My father was a man of integrity and a good provider, but what we now call quality time did not exist between us. Soon I came to expect and perceive rejection everywhere. My own bitter root judgment was the assumption, based on the perception that my father rejected me – that I must look ugly!

(As Abbot David Geraets of the Spiritual Directors School taught, "Children are great observers, but poor interpreters)." This is because most children have good eyesight, excellent hearing, but insufficient life experience to make prudent, supportable judgements based on all the relevant facts.

As a result, my habit was routinely to withdraw from social contact, preferring seclusion to the pain of rejection; my constant expectation. I was almost 18 before I had the courage to invite a girl on a date, then rarely did so – because I was ugly!

No wonder I was called egg-head, stuffed shirt, arrogant, stuck up, self-important and a lot worse in high school; the assumption was that I thought I was too good for them, children mostly of sugar cane farmers and merchants. All those names heaped additional psychological pain on top of my self-assessment of being ugly. The names continually strengthened my bitter root judgement and withdrawal from social events – certainly I was ugly!

It was the acceptance and love of my bride that healed me at age 26. At that time I was able to accept that I must be just ordinary.

It is not just that we occasionally are actually rejected. Our own interpretation of events is critical. Too often, we perceive rejection where none was intended by the other. For instance, someone may reject us as a possible spouse, but not as a good friend. We withdraw not based on actual rejection, but on our interpretation of events. In effect, our own decisions, based in self-doubt lead us into self-rejection. Even an unthinking comment might be seen by some as a rejection.

We do it to ourselves while blaming others. While we think we are being rejected according to the intent of another, actually we are rejecting the other who had no such intent".

In summary? It is our own attitude, left over from childhood disappointments that too often control us. We are our own worst enemy. As Pogo, the cartoon 'possum once said, "We have met the enemy and he is us!"

Ronda also mentioned the "wounded healer." The concept often is mentioned in active Church circles. It is based on the famous book by Henri Nouwen, *The Wounded Healer*. The idea is this, often observed in reality. One who is repeatedly subjected in childhood or youth – whether really or only by perception – to the same negative experience often will develop a bitter root judgment related to that negative experience. We are well aware of Ronda's bitter root judgement.

However! No one else better understands the problem and consequence of their own negative experience; the resulting bitter root judgment. Many who have suffered in youth spend much of their adult life as "wounded healers" helping others overcome the same type of negative experience and self-judgment that plagued themselves. A few examples will speak louder than more explanatory verbiage.

Example: my wife lost both parents in childhood. She was bounced around in several foster homes before she landed in the house of Ed and Marilyn Bond: good, serious, supportive people. My wife spent much of her adult life ministering to the young, especially foster or abandoned street children and those incarcerated. She received an award for her work with incarcerated teens as a wounded healer.

Example: As to myself, I avoid the appearance of rejecting others by constantly seeking to affirm everyone I meet in my work as a commander, manager, evangelist, retreat master, author and spiritual director; a wounded healer in action.

Example: Ronda, herself, despite her issues, is a wounded healer; writing books and organizing workshops helpful to resolving women's issues.

Returning to Ronda's journal.

May 13: Ronda: Anxiety about editing this manuscript. More feelings of joy, thanksgiving and peace. Better on finger picking.

May 14. Ronda: I awoke slightly anxious about the new chapters in the Escaping Anxiety book and the new radio show. I give this to you, Jesus, rebuking any evil spirit hovering around these projects. Take them away.

Jesus - It is because you are seeing it all from the human standpoint. I will bring the good. Surrender it all to me.

May 15: Ronda: I woke up this morning full of joy and a sense that Jesus wants me to witness here in Corpus Christi to other widows about dedicated widowhood, and that thinking of "the other possibility" as allowed by His permissive will, was to put me in greater solidarity with other widows.

Spiritual Director's commentary: Ronda has mentioned joy. It is as much a hope as a reality at this point. Real, perhaps, but passing. We will continue to report the ongoing battle for detachment, while moving on to the definition and explanation of unconditional charity, i.e., unconditional love. That is the last step.

Authentic, complete detachment as defined and explained, yields peace without anxiety. Unconditional love yields the long sought constant spiritual joy. The final quest. *Ad Majorem Dei Gloriam.*

For Personal Reflection and Group Sharing:

- What is your worst or recurring actual nightmare in sleep, or "nightmare" in your fantasies of worst possibility?

- How can you pray better at such times based on insights in this session?

Session XIII – Lost River and the Way Back

Those who see the will of God in the smallest things or in the most distressing and fatal events accept them all with equal joy, gladness, and respect. What other people fear and fly from in horror is received by them with honor.

Abandonment to Divine Providence, Jean-Pierre de Caussade

Spiritual Director's Introduction: We will continue to report on Ronda's struggle to detach from her dominating will to control; but the final cure comes with the next, final step to sustained spiritual joy. That last step is unconditional charity, or love. In the Catholic understanding, charity includes not only monetary generosity, but all forms of selfless, spiritual love as expressed in their proper time and place.

Regarding the definition of *unconditional* charity, Ronda knew that was coming next, often mentioned in our conversations. She said, "I have a feeling we are talking past each other. That you mean something like loving people without demanding something in return from them; while I mean something like excusing all their sins.

The traditional definition of spiritual love is "wanting the best for another." It is somewhere in the Catechism. God loves us as we are – sins and all. He wills and offers the best for us, but not by force. He gave us free will and we have the power to resist or disobey. We can deny His will and suffer the consequences.

Similarly, with a stranger, friend, spouse, brother, sister, son or daughter, you want the best for them, but cannot force it upon them. They, too, have free will and despite your best efforts they have their own idea of what is best or desired by them – wrong-headed as they might be.

You may force a young child to do the right thing as a manner of training, but adults are free. If they choose the wrong, they live with the consequences. If the consequences don't teach them – as hard as it might seem – that is their problem, not yours. At some point you have to "let go and let God!"

Unconditional charity is always to love: "hate the sin, love the sinner." AND KEEP THESE TWO, THE

SIN AND THE SINNER, SEPARATE IN YOUR MIND AND HEART.

Insight: St Benedict told his abbots, "If the monks do evil and you have not instructed or chastised them, you are responsible for their behavior. If they do evil and you have instructed or chastised them, you bear no guilt (are not complicit)".

Unconditional charity is love of God and all mankind always and without exception. This includes active works of love and passive, in the heart authentic love as defined above. Unconditionally! This is a realizable goal once detachment of will is assured. (The above does not negate the need for balance in one's life, born of authentic prudence, even to killing an enemy in self-defense; all the same praying for the enemy).

To the extent you live unconditional charity, you unite yourself with the living God who is unconditional love. As we tell the children, "God is love."

We return to Ronda's journal with this understanding: full detachment destroys anxiety. Full detachment is the door and key down the hall of unconditional charity to the open door of constant joy.

+

May 1: Ronda:

I am remembering a healing image concerning

father rejection. I like to tell people who don't under-stand the benefits to the parishioners of having a priest celebrating mass for them every day, if they can come:

My father left us when we were kids and we were anxious about money for food, but when I became a Catholic I got thousands of men called father who lay down their lives to bring us our celestial food at holy mass.

My daughter, Carla, is having greater suffering and fears of return of lymphoma. I asked God to give it all to me to suffer instead of her. I saw it was a concern, but that I needed to rebuke the spirit of obsessive anxiety and accept whatever will be the permissive will of Jesus in this surrendering Carla into His heart.

May 16: Ronda: I was anxious about time zone issues on a radio show I was doing. I kept obsessing because even to call to ask ahead could be too early, Pacific time. I kept trying (to calm down). It was a legitimate concern, but I still was overly anxious. So I decided to call even if it would be 7am Pacific time. I got a good answer!

This shows how taking action is usually better than just speculating. This same method worked again with anxiety about Richard's surgery. Into your heart, dear Jesus, I commend dear Richard.

Jesus - Just as a mother watches her toddler first

fall every few steps, then gradually less and less, when I am teaching you through a spiritual director how to improve, I am not alarmed that you still make many, many mistakes. I just want you to hold my hand more and try again.

Al: Remember this locution. It still applies.

May 16/17: Ronda's Midnight Image

You who fear rejection:

Not by grabbing,

Trying to capture,

Locking the door...

Come inside

My heart

Where I make all to be one.

Al: That is the whole point of my spiritual direction and the source of all joy. To be all as one in Christ is true charity and resultant joy. At the right time, I could write a whole chapter (or a book?) based on your midnight image.

May 18: Ronda: Lots of little free floating anxieties – seems to be mitigated by coffee, meals, and immediate "Take away the spirit of excessive anxiety, dear Jesus" prayers.

Horrible scene yelling at a person who seemed to be rejecting me by rejecting that I think Jesus speaks to me in interior locutions. Al was present and he thinks that I did much better, catching myself after one yell, stopping and apologizing.

Spiritual Director's comment: Seated at the opposite end of the table, I saw it coming. The face tells all! In sequence the unease, the ire, the angry reaction of assumed rejection welling up, the Ronda volcano ready to explode. But she caught it and calmed. Progress!

May 19: Ronda: Glitches with (my radio program), but instead of getting anxious and angry, I slowly did what I could to remedy the glitches!! Thank you, Jesus, for making me an instrument of your love.

Al: Instrument of love? Just working out a problem? How so? This is love of God: To accept and deal with the present moment (which God has permitted) rather than go on another fruitless tirade against a reality which God has permitted. She anticipates an element of unconditional love! In effect she has obeyed the command of God in the present moment!

May 20: Ronda: Two family crises. I am concerned, trying not to escalate into excessive anxiety even though these are serious. I surrender those involved into your heart, dear Jesus, and call upon friends who can give good advice.

Feeling depressed because of family concerns. Played Schubert on the You-tube and cleared out drawers. That felt good.

May 21: Ronda: I woke up anxious about the book, thinking it was too short, not enough context, not enough description. I anxiously cogitated about this before even thinking the anxiety was an example of obsessing vs. normal concern.

So now, Jesus, I place in your hands our book on anxiety. Take away my obsessive anxiety. Make us instruments of Your love, not rushing just to be finished!

It was a good meeting of the minds with Al. We are agreed on manuscript improvements. Thank you, Jesus.

I was slightly anxious about my RondaView program, but it went well with two new panelists, the old ones making great strides with the challenges of the first week.

Jesus - See? You are overly anxious, while things often go well.

Ronda: I decided to try the challenge of talking to You, my Jesus, all day for a week even if I don't get words in the heart that easily can be recorded.

Al: There is great precedence in this as a way to joy and holiness. Blessed Brother Lawrence was a French monk stuck working in the monastery kitchen for 20 years. Could not go to prayers with the community. So he talked with Jesus among the pots and pans and market shopping on a near continuous basis. He became so holy that the vicar of the King would not summon the holy monk to the castle for advice but got in his carriage and went to the monastery for consultation. We know of Blessed Brother Lawrence through the many letters of spiritual advice he sent to directees throughout France.

May 22: Ronda: I awoke terrified. I thought I could lose all three of my children before I left this earth!

Jesus - Ronda, you must suffer with them on their crosses as my mother Mary and Mary Magdalene did, also perpetually putting them into my crucified heart.

Note to the reader: Ronda received terrible news regarding her daughters and was in an agonizing state for a couple of days, until it became clear that the news was greatly exaggerated.

Spiritual Director's Comment: This is holiness – to live in the present moment, neither regretting the past, nor being anxious about the future, but existing only for the present moment as gift. And to respond to the gift with unconditional love centered on the needs of the present moment. Easy to write, more challenging to live.

But that is not to declare myself holy, for two reasons. First, to do so is against humility, the foundational virtue; and more importantly for the reader, understand this reality; holiness is not a place or an accomplishment, but a goal and a process. There always is a higher path up the holy mountain of God. You and I struggle on.

If you seriously want to struggle on to the pinnacle of holiness, go to the appendix now, read it and return to session 14. Then read, no, study the appendix again and again until you fully understand. Then you will choose one of four alternatives. The first alternative is to do nothing. You can start that now if you wish. The other three call for understandings and actions I recommend in the appendix.

All are called to holiness, few achieve it. As Jesus says, *"Enter through the narrow gate; for the gate is wide and the road easy that leads to destruction, and there are many who take it. For the gate is narrow and the road is hard that leads to life, and there are few who find it.* (Matt: 7: 13, 14.)

For Personal Reflection and Group Sharing

- How were you challenged by Al Hughes' teaching on unconditional love?

- Go through a week keeping a journal of experiences of excessive anxiety and how these were overcome by the prayer that you have been practicing in line with the themes of this book.

Session XIV

Rounding Bayou Bend

"God... finds no purer disposition in... His...(child) than this entire self-renunciation for the sake of living the life of grace according to the divine operation..."

Jean-Pierre De Caussade

Spiritual Director's Introduction: There is good news to relate. Yes, Ronda continues to have setbacks, but that is to be expected. She is fighting a personal control addiction: excessive control in the face of God and man, borne of a fear of ultimate rejection.

But here is the good news. To an increasing degree, she is self-analyzing her feelings and behavior, recognizing missteps more quickly, recovering more quickly at the first hint of anger, integrating the healing concepts we have discussed, and consistently is becoming more relaxed, even cheerful unto joy-

143

fulness at times. *And,* she has self-discovered the role melancholic pessimism has played in her habitual anxieties. Proud of her! She got ahead of me on that one!

There is, among Christians, a commonly heard phrase, "Let Go, and let God." It is good and true advice, but not very helpful to understanding. Instead, we use and explain three words or phrases which get more to the point: detachment, abandonment, and self-renunciation. They are essentially interchangeable as used here.

By whichever word or phrase you prefer, the hard truth is that you cannot be fully obedient to the will of God if still you are attached to inordinate desire for any of the things of creation – including your own will. Nor can you be obedient to God if you spend your time regretting the past or fearing the future. God is in the eternal present. But if you are all in for the will of God and are unconditional in your charity, there is where you may find union with God.

In this session and as presented in the appendix, with the help of de Caussade, I will try to describe what union with God is like.

For now, we look in on Ronda's struggle and progress. Notice the role of pessimism she has discovered and her efforts to integrate various concepts from other sources into a whole of functional understanding.

May 24. Ronda: I am seeing how anxiety is related to pessimism and that I have to come against such melancholic pessimism since at least 50% of the time things turn out well. What is needed is not optimism but realism and hope.

I awoke in the night with noxious feelings, I kept rebuking them and finally went to sleep. This morning it seems as if Jesus is telling me that such episodes are part of how He wants me to be interceding for all those in sin and confusion.

I was concerned about my daughters, but both are doing better than I thought. Again, I should be less pessimistic.

Pessimistic about a visit to a high prelate... (Meeting him) I loved him and was very encouraged by him to have faith and hope amidst different possibilities for the future in the Church. Jesus seemed to smile at me and say, "See, I surprised you."

May 25. Jesus - When waves of anxiety come over you regarding different matters in the Church, always rebuke the spirit of anxiety and ask Me to give you courage not to expend energy in anxiety, speculation. Cling to me in the Eucharist and prayer.

Ronda: I am remembering a directive from Recovery International (not 12 step), Dr. Abraham Low's institute for out of control emotions. I was part of this for twenty years. (They taught) "Take a secure

145

thought."

This means that when one is anxious one should think of something concerning the matter (of concern) that would help you become more secure. For example, I am anxious because I will be late to a meeting. I can take the secure thought that when I get there my associates will quickly summarize what has gone on before in my absence.

On a natural level this is helpful, though it needs to be combined with trust in God's providence.

With regard to certain Church issues, I am taking the secure thought that I know many priests and other leaders who know more than I about these issues and who will have good suggestions on how to handle complicated situations that may arise.

May 26. Ronda: In spite of the good advice of Jesus, I got into excessive speculation about possible Church matters, leading to hours of excessive anxiety! It feels like a set-back!

Jesus - When you give into the temptation to worry and speculate and try to scheme to avoid suffering in the future, then you feel terrible. Notice how terrible you feel, and come back into My heart, where alone is security.

Ronda: I accept Your permissive will.... (I took a nap and woke up with that glorious peaceful feeling. Thank you, Jesus). Later, I was thinking pessimistically about a group I run, thinking that it would fold because the women wouldn't come and all the reasons why it isn't working, etc. But they did come and obviously are benefiting! More excessive anxiety. Sigh.

May 27. Ronda: This morning I awoke with a steady, sweet, tender spiritual joy in my heart. It is now three hours later and it is still there. It is an unusual day in that I have nothing that I have to do except receive a Skype call later. I read this in De Caussade, *Abandonment to Divine Providence,* book 2, Chapter 1, Section 1. (Christian treasury, on-line).

"God, who finds no purer disposition in His spouse than this entire self-renunciation for the sake of living the life of grace according to the divine operation, provides her with necessary books, thoughts, insight into her own soul, advice and counsel, and the examples of the wise. Everything that others discover with great difficulty this soul finds in abandonment, and what they guard with care in order to be able to fine it again, this soul receives at the moment there is occasion for it and afterwards relinquishes so as to admit nothing but exactly what God desires it to have on order to live by Him alone.

Ronda continues: I am thinking that maybe God is giving me less structured work, precisely to bring me to this point? Your thoughts, Al?

Al: The best way I can interpret that quote of De

Caussade is to share my own first experience of this.

Partial quote: "*God ...provides...necessary books, thoughts, insight, advice and counsel, and the examples of the wise. Everything that others discover with great difficulty this soul finds in abandonment, and what they guard with care in order to be able to fine it again, this soul receives at the moment there is occasion for it....*"

I first noticed this while writing my third book. First of all, I had no topic in mind and was not particularly keen to start another book. But then, by no effort of my own, a title was impressed upon my mind. Sporadically, over the next few weeks, chapter titles were given me, in a clear and logical sequence. Among them were topics for which I had no clue.

But I started writing. Every time (and often) I encountered a need for which I had no clue, the need was satisfied by *necessary books, thoughts, insight, advice and counsel, and the examples of the wise.* None of this acquired by my own efforts.

May 28. Ronda: On the way to Holy Mass, I twitted Al about something. Then all through Mass I was excessively anxious thinking he might reject me because of my sassiness. After Mass, I realized that I needed to apologize.

To my surprise, he wasn't annoyed at all, took what I said as teasing. We both realized it was a sterling example of over anxiousness and the need to clear up what causes it. Of course, my bitter root is the irrational fear of rejection!

Something came up in conversation with Al involving doing something imprudent that could lead to broken bones. Al said these can be preludes in old age to an earlier death than otherwise. Here is the rest of that amazing conversation.

Ronda continues: So, if you knew for sure you would go to heaven immediately after you died, would you still want to live on earth longer?

Al: Yes, because my life on earth is heaven!

Ronda: Even though St. Catherine of Siena, a doctor of the Church, says that "all the way to heaven is heaven," I don't think she meant what Al meant, but I could be wrong. I think she meant that all the graces we experience on the way are a participation in Heaven.

I long for heaven and can't wait to leave this earth on the basis that purgatory is better than life on earth because we will know we are saved. I can't imagine ever saying I wanted to stay on this earth longer because my life here is heaven. Please clarify, dear Al.

Al: Ronda didn't say it, but we were talking about the joy of riding motorcycles. Not prudent at our age. If we had to lay one down, broken bones will not heal so fast and can lead to life threatening complications.

So I was talking about the new three wheel cycles now on the market!

Anyway, I am not going to argue with St. Catherine. Just agree. And, along the lines of St. Paul's comment, he was indifferent: to stay awhile or to go. To stay was to continue to witness to the glory of God. To go, he anticipated paradise and the end to suffering.

I for one am delighted to find myself in God's corner on the basis of detachment and unconditional love. Rather than anxiety, joy. Rather than self-absorption, evangelization. Rather than hate, love. Rather than compete, cooperate and build up. Rather than criticize, help and affirm. Rather than drudgery, joyful fulfillment of my call. Rather than regret, harvest wisdom from suffering. Rather than anticipate, rejoice in the next delightful surprise from God. I already live in paradise, just a different mansion. *Eye has not seen, nor ear heard....*

For Personal Reflection and Group Sharing:

- *How would you describe any progress in, through grace, escaping from anxiety on the road to spiritual joy, since you started reading this book?*

Session XV

From the Top of the Levee

They who have my commandments and keep them are those who love me; and those who love me will be loved by my Father, and I will love them and reveal myself to them. (John 14:21)

We began anxiously entering the dismal swamp at dusk: a dark, foreboding place of twisting channels, overhanging terrors, choked narrowing passageways, and switchbacks leading nowhere. As someone else wrote, the silence of darkest night was punctuated by *sounds and fury signifying nothing*. Signifying nothing but fear, anger, rage, death of soul. Uncontrolled terror of abandonment and loss. We challenged the beast that dwells in the reeds, dug deep for roots of obstruction, searched for the way home. Lost in darkness.

But too, it is written, *"The Son also rises."* From here at the top of the levee, in the full daylight cast by the Son, we look back at the swamp. Discover its beauty. In the dark, there was only sudden frights and death. Here in the light, only life and discovery. Ronda is on her way home. The Father awaits. She shall be secure.

Have you seen the video? Carl Jung, the famous research psychologist was interviewed at length by a young man shortly before he passed. At the very end, Carl was asked, "Do you believe in God?"

Calmly, he answered, "No." Letting that sink in, in silence. As a little grin spread across his face he then said, "I don't believe in Him, I know Him."

Consider that banner quotation at the head of this last session.

> *They who have my commandments and keep them are those who love me; ...*

Historically, the Israelites took the Ten Commandments and converted them into six hundred plus rules to define holiness. We are often no better. We add explanation upon explanation into vast libraries, attempting to define holiness. Yet holiness can be defined, as did Jesus, completely in one short phrase. "Not as I will, but as Thou wilt."

"And those who love me will be loved by my Father..." This is the lesson of the quotation. The love of God is expressed by obedience to the Father's will. It is all so simple! Detach, be love and obey! It is all so

simple!

As I sat in my usual chair last evening listening to Jazz Happening Now, drinking two fingers of Zaya Trinidad rum, maraschino cherry bathed in elixir, Session XV wrote itself in the hidden hallways of my subconscious mind, where God speaks.

"...and I will love them and reveal myself to them". If, rather than believe in God, you desire to know Him, you now know the way. You have the map. By following it you will *Escape Anxiety along the Road to Spiritual Joy.*

If you make it near the end of the road, you will understand why I could say to Ronda, "Yes, because my life on earth is heaven!" With Carl Jung I can say, "I don't believe in Him, I know Him." I see him in the stream of graces, gifts He provides as I try to fulfill His will. I hear him and try to obey. It is as De Caussade wrote. Life is effortless and joyful in His will. Detach, be love and obey.

TO KNOW AND NOT TO DO, IS NOT YET TO KNOW.

+

So how is Ronda doing? For one last time, let us return to her journal.

May 29: Jesus - See how I surround you with protectors? The sanctified Ronda would still be

Russian/Jewish/Spanish ancestry in your personality. You would not become tranquil Al, just more peaceful because more trusting.

May 30: Ronda: During the night, hard to sleep with anxious thoughts about Carla who seems to think she is dying, as on the prayer meeting on-line she seemed to be saying goodbye to all of us bravely and beautifully. I am anxious about whether to go to her since she doesn't want me to come when she is in bad pain but only if she is dying. But my twin, her aunt to whom she is very close, offered to come to comfort her and she said to wait until more news of the diagnosis.

During the night, I kept bringing Carla in prayer into the heart of Jesus.

I awoke more resigned to whatever will be the permissive will of God in Carla's future, and determined to avoid excessive anxiety in all of this I can't control, just offering all the pain of it to Jesus, like Mary at the foot of the Cross.

Al: Ronda? Oh, yes. She is doing just fine. *Ad Majorem Dei Gloriam!*

We praise God by recalling His marvelous deeds. (Cassiodorus)

Ronda's Final Words to the Reader

"Love has no room for fear; rather, perfect love casts out all fear...love is not yet perfect in one who is afraid. We, for our part, love because He first loved us." (1 John 4:)

Here is my description of how I escaped from anxiety along the road to spiritual joy. I believe that Jesus, my bridegroom as a dedicated widow, worked through Al Hughes to direct me along this road.

Highlights of this journey are these:

- Learning to distinguish between normal concerns and excessive anxiety.

- Through allowing my director into the most hellish pits of my psyche, he could lead me to discover the bitter root, the deepest causes of my excessive anxiety.

- This gave my director a chance to work on healing strategies. If you recall, in the introduction Al Hughes writes about how the spiritual director does not just give advice but enters into the very heart of the directee. Instead of rejecting me when he had to see me at my worst, he showed me unconditional love.

- Gradually, we developed steps I could take in daily life whenever I identified excessive anxiety. (These steps are listed for the benefit of the readers at the end of this chapter.)

- After six months of intensive spiritual direction at our weekly formal session, but also on car drives to Mass, and other encounters, I now believe that I am well along the road to spiritual joy. Anxiety is no longer my usual default state of mind. More and more there is lightness and often felt spiritual joy.

This prayer-poem seems to me to crystallize what I want to convey to you, the reader, about the process you have just finished reading about:

Spiritual Mentor

Your eyes

from looking

only at God

no longer mirror

the world.

I look at them

and I see

not a tiny miniature

of my outer self

but only God's love.

Steps to Take when Feeling Anxiety

1. Ask yourself, do I have a legitimate concern or is this excessive anxiety?

2. If it is excessive anxiety, do not linger in that state, for it will become like quicksand. Pray immediately when feeling anxious: "I rebuke the spirit of excessive anxiety and lay it at Your feet, dear Jesus. Take it away!"

3. Try to recall any bitter root judgments causing anxiety coming from your childhood.

4. Pray: I accept whatever You permit for my next day, next week, next month, next year...for all the rest of my life on earth.

5. Pray: I surrender my anxiety about this person, or this circumstance, or this possible event, into Your heart.

6. If you have bad habits that manifest your excessive anxiety, ask your guardian angel to remind you that you are exhibiting them so you can stop!

Other Steps you have tried that work:

_____

_____

_____

Appendix

So You Want a Spiritual Director?

Congratulations! The first possibility is to do nothing. And that is what you likely would get. Nothing but your life's business as usual. But you want more. I hope you want more passionately! But be alert. There is conflict ahead: two camps within the Catholic Church, one that certainly will lead you astray.

There are those who are magisterial in outlook. That is to say, they believe and follow the teachings of Christ, the Apostles, the Church. And from holy spiritual writers; in a nutshell, the traditions of the Church. From them comes the understandings and practice of holiness. Among them you may find ways to increased holiness.

But there are some whose desire is to "modernize" the Church, meaning primarily to accept selected morals and mores of secular influence in our time, replacing the discipline and freedom of Christ with the licentiousness of more hedonistic desires. They generally oppose ancient Church teachings and will lead you away from holiness. Keep that in mind!

For each of the three remaining alternatives to be suggested, you need to consider four issues regarding your quest:

- Determine which alternative is best at this stage of your life
- Determine how to find the right help.
- Determine, through a few visits the compatibility of the proposed guide.
- Determine your desired goals.

Spiritual Directors will want to know your answers to questions such as these:

- Have you received baptism, confirmation and Eucharist, remaining in good standing as an adult in the Catholic Church? Registered with a parish?
- Do you attend Mass every Sunday, excepting illness or inability to find a church (travel status)?
- Do you go to confession at least monthly? More often as necessary?
- If possible, do you go to Mass and receive the host worthily several times a week?
- Do you have an active daily prayer practice?

First alternative: follow a magisterial friend, not a priest, who agrees to mentor you.

Your best bet may be this alternative. Find Christ first in community. Choose a mentor who is a lay member, consecrated Sister or Brother, who knows you well and is able to answer yes to all those above questions about their Catholic practice.

Learn the finer points of Catholic life from your mentor.

As to competence, an active Catholic mentor whom you believe to be holier than yourself is the minimum required. Your goal should be personal growth in both knowledge and practice of the faith.

Second alternative: seek a parish priest mentor who can meet you regularly.

Keep in mind that priests are people, too. The good and the not so good. And that some are magisterial and some are not. Should you find one willing to meet with you, say weekly or monthly, there is another problem. Parish priests who say yes to your request for a spiritual director may not be able to give you the time and insights needed. They can lead you toward holiness.

Third alternative: seek a fully qualified order priest or a fully trained lay spiritual director.

Generally, such a person will be recommended by former and present directees as being him/herself holy, prudent, and compassionate.

+

Your ultimate goal is expressed by De Caussade in this way:

"When God lives in the soul, it ought to abandon itself entirely to His providences. When God lives in the soul, it has nothing left of self, but only that which the spirit which actuates it imparts to it at each moment. Nothing is provided for the future, no road is marked out, but it is like a child which can be led wherever one pleases, and has only feeling to distinguish what is presented to it....for God allows it no other support than that which He gives it Himself."

True holiness only requires full detachment in favor of the will of God and unconditional charity. With the guidance of a trained spiritual director, God will provide the rest as you find Him in your soul. You will remain in union with Him.

Necessarily, this has been a brief survey. You may wish to read next, *Abandonment to Divine Providence* by Jean-Pierre de Caussade (on-line free)

The Most High is closer than you think. May you find Him in your soul.

Ad Majorem Dei Gloriam. Albert E. Hughes, Spiritual Director.